PINAFORE STREET

PINAFORE STREET

STREET

A Fenland childhood

KATHLEEN LORD

Dedicated to my son, David.

ISBN
1 901253 39 2
First published March 2004

British Library Cataloguing in Publication Data.
A catalogue record for this book
is available from the British Library

Published by:
Léonie Press
an imprint of
Anne Loader Publications
13 Vale Road, Hartford,
Northwich, Cheshire CW8 1PL Gt Britain
Tel: 01606 75660   Fax: 01606 77609
e-mail: anne@leoniepress.com
Website: www.anneloaderpublications.co.uk
www.leoniepress.com

Printed by:
Anne Loader Publications
Collated and bound by: B & S Swindells Ltd, Knutsford
Covers laminated by: The Finishing Touch, St Helens

iv

Kathleen Lord

About the Author

Kathleen Lord was born in 1914, the eldest child of Annie and Albert Hall. Her mother was orphaned at six and worked in a Boston cigar factory before marrying. Albert's family farmed for generations at Ingoldsby, Lincolnshire. He was 13 when his father died, and his mother later became a midwife at Boston, where Albert joined the building trade. Eventually, 'Grandma Hall' and Albert's six brothers and sisters settled in Manchester.

Kathleen was a serious child who absorbed everything going on around her. She excelled at English and swimming. At 19 she left home to become secretary to an architect in Barn Hill, Stamford, opposite a solicitor's office. One of the young clerks there, Frederick Lord, became her husband. After qualifying to teach shorthand and typewriting, she trained several generations of students at evening classes.

These memoirs were written when she retired in the 1970s. She still lives in south Lincolnshire.

This book was originally called "Pinafore Street" because when it was written in the 1970s the author did not want to pinpoint her childhood home too clearly, to avoid giving unwitting offence to anyone mentioned in its pages.

However we have persuaded her that it will have much more historical significance if she reveals that she actually lived in Freiston Road, Boston – and we doubt that anyone will be other than pleased to have been recorded in this delightful book.

We have kept the original title.

Anne and Jack Loader
Léonie Press
January 2004

Contents

*Kathleen with her parents, Annie and Albert Hall.
She was born on April 15, 1914.*

Chapter 1

NUMBER 10

We moved into Number 10 Pinafore Street[1] when I was about four and a half years old. It was the end house of a row of four two-up and two-down cottages which stood back from the street behind little squares of front garden. A dirt and cinder passageway ran alongside our house and two side gates led off it – one to give access to the front door and the other opening into a small yard-cum-garden at the rear.

The property was not tumbledown, but all four rooms were claustrophobically small and there was a box staircase which went up behind a wooden partition wall in the living room. This staircase was a death trap unless the door at the bottom was left ajar, or one of the bedroom doors was open to emit light from the bedroom windows. If someone forgot and closed the doors at top and bottom, it became a black tunnel which filled me with a suffocating fear whenever I found myself shut in. Unwary relatives, who came to stay with us, fumbled and stumbled unless they were fore-warned. It was particularly dangerous when leaving the bedrooms for there was no square footage at the top and one was confronted in each doorway with a black void beyond the first two or three risers.

Two cupboards filled the small recesses either side of the cottage grate in the living room. In one we kept our collection of crockery, the rent book, insurance man's card, other outgoing records and odds and ends. The cupboard on the other side served as a pantry. I do not remember lack of space in it being any great embarrassment, though my mother performed daily miracles on the table with what came out of it.

All cooking was done on the coal fire or in the tiny oven at the right-hand side. At the other side was the hot water boiler with a bright brass tap protruding from its stomach. Mother was always afraid of it going dry and blowing up, and anyone who took water from it was warned to be sure to replenish it with cold water AT ONCE. That was not so easy. The cold water tap – which all four houses shared – stood in its sacking glory in the front garden of the house next door. The water-carrier had to journey down the passageway and out onto the street, or in Father's case, through the parlour into the front garden, and perform a contortionist's act with the bucket over the dividing fence. The procedure became even more of a farce during a spell of severe frost for then the hot water from the boiler had to be used to thaw the tap before the bucket could be filled to replenish the boiler.

The front parlour was the width of the stairs wider than the living room, which made it almost square. It was a pleasant little room, looking out onto the garden and the street. There was an old-fashioned corner cupboard angled high up on the wall near the door leading into the living room, and its carved and glass-panelled front protected and displayed Mother's little collection of bric-à-brac. This room housed all that she held dear, but we had no love for it. The leather-seated chairs, festooned with pink and green crocheted antimacassars, were cold to our bottoms. The variegated aspidistra on its tall stand in the window was a toppling menace when we wanted to see outside. The pair of bulbous china vases and matching clock with their painted panels of frolicking shepherds and shepherdesses filled the narrow imitation white-marble mantelpiece and blocked our view in the mirror, even when we teetered on the rail of the brass fender. In short, it was a "thou shalt not touch" room and it never came alive for us except around Christmastime when our tinselled tree ousted the aspidistra, or when someone called whom Mother thought was important enough to be entertained in it.

The passageway wound round behind our coal-house and privy and served as a rear entrance to the other three houses. It also gave rear access to several other houses which backed up to ours and whose frontages faced onto a broad footpath running alongside the Maud Foster Drain.[2]

Our backyard was enclosed on both sides by low brick walls, and an uneven brick path led to the outhouses at the bottom. The privy was the bane of my poor mother's life and the scene of one of her most embarrassing moments. She 'couldn't abide dirt' and the wooden seat, and its wooden lids which fitted the two graded holes, were scrubbed and scoured regularly. The brick walls and wooden roof supports were lime-washed every spring. Fly papers hung above our heads in summertime and a small seaside bucket, minus its handle, stood filled with a pink powder disinfectant and had an old tablespoon sticking up in it. We ladled out a spoonful of the powder and sprinkled it down the hole whenever we paid a visit. It was always a refuge if I wanted to avoid an errand or be out of harm's way after some devilishness. I sat comfortably behind the bolted door on the smaller hole, with the lid clamped down on its neighbour close beside me and lost myself reading *Tiger Tim* or *Chatterbox*. The strong odour of the disinfectant and the buzzing of captive flies struggling against tacky odds were accepted as part of the price one had to pay.

One day my mother paid a visit and was sitting peacefully, when she became conscious of a draught of cool air coming up through the hole. To her horror a male voice said: "Don't mind me missis, I'll leave yours until I've done the next one." It was the dillyman with his spade and grab who had opened the small wooden trapdoor at the foot of the rear wall. She never forgot the incident and for years afterwards it was more than any of us dare to mention it. In later years, he and his kind became Night Soil Men and grabbed and shovelled by the light of the moon and swinging lanterns – to the accompaniment of slamming bedroom windows!

---

[1] 'Number 10': No. 10 Freiston Road, Boston, Lincolnshire

[2] Drain: man-made waterway to prevent fenland from flooding

Chapter 2

NEIGHBOURS

The houses nearby were a mixture. Some were as small as ours but thrust their windows to the edge of the pavement. Others were decidedly class-conscious semis and boasted long, narrow lawns. Here and there, sandwiched between their meaner neighbours were the singles, yet even this select minority could rarely boast a bathroom, and the dillymen emptied the ash privies once a week. Cars and garages were the perquisites of the wealthy and we knew nothing at all about them. The majority of the back gardens housed bicycles – 'usables' and 'has-beens' – in sheds or propped beneath kitchen windows, shrouded for protection under cast-off clothing or old bedding. Our immediate neighbours on the other side of the passageway were hidden from us at the rear by a very high brick wall and the house, which was much larger than ours, stood up to the pavement so that its bulk threw a perpetual shadow across our little front garden. This annoyed my mother who loved growing flowers, especially pansies. Few of the things she planted survived, partly through lack of sunshine and partly because there were several luxurious clumps of fern in which slugs and snails lurked until her back was turned.

I was very curious about this house over the wall, because the front downstairs window was permanently shuttered. There was a large family of children and I soon got to know them and solved the riddle. It had been a fish shop and the pans were still there with their lids raised, and the fat from the final night's frying was still in them, rancid, foul-smelling and growing a 'fur coat'. The business had been transferred to a lock-up shop at the far end of the street, though fish was still cut up and potatoes prepared for chipping in the back-yard behind the high wall. Everybody in our row knew about it when the wind was in the right direction. It didn't trouble me though. I loved to go round there and I dodged my mother whenever I could. We did exactly as we liked. There were seven children, six girls and a boy, with a big, slow-moving, phlegmatic father and a delicate mother. We played and squabbled and scratched ourselves to our heart's content. The rag rug and lino on the floor of the living room were greasy and dun-coloured. There was nothing to spoil. The cat jumped up on the torn leather settee and vanished through a hole into the stuffing to sleep out of the way of our scuffling feet. When I got back home, out came the dreaded fine-toothed comb, the hair brush and shoulder drape, and I was de-loused, de-nitted and deodorized mercilessly. Mother was forever on the hunt and there were quite a few times when I didn't disappoint her.

Her threat of the school nurse's lopping scissors if she found 'livestock', or that I should have to go there smelling of nit-killer fell on deaf ears, and in the end she shrugged her shoulders and hoped for the best.

It was in that house that I first met death. The last born

was a boy and though he only lived for a few weeks he made quite a name for himself. He was the subject of much talk amongst the old folk in the neighbourhood because he had been born with several fully developed first teeth which they said was an ill omen, believing he would grow up with a belligerent nature and even murderous tendencies! So he probably saved himself and his parents a 'peck of trouble' later on by falling into an early decline and passing away one Sunday morning. A day or so afterwards, my boisterous playmates led me up the dingy staircase into the front bedroom, past the double bed with its corner knobs askew, to a gloomy recess by its side. So that I should not miss the teeth, one of them dashed across to the window and pulled aside a faded paper blind which had been drawn down in respect of the dead. There lay the baby, teeth and all, in a small white coffin which looked extraordinarily like an outsize shoebox. One of the family, believing the old saying that if you do not touch the body, you will dream about it, grabbed one of my hands and pressed my grimy palm down onto the still little face. It was icy and I was terrified. My hand felt numb with shock for a long while afterwards. I never told my mother but I know she was puzzled during the next few days by my repeated requests for some water to wash my hands in, please.

The house adjoining was exactly like our own, except that it had a wooden lean-to at the back. This gave enough room for a gas stove and for the mangle to be used under cover. My mother was frankly envious and a year or two later when the house became vacant, we moved in, over the garden wall.

The couple who had lived there were middle-aged and childless and always at loggerheads with one another. Mother blamed the wallpaper in the living room – it was pillarbox red. My father found a fishing friend in the man, and mother an inveterate gossip in his wife. It was always "he" and "she" when they referred to each other in conversation with us. What they called one another indoors was quite different. I told my mother what it was once, and she boxed my ears. "He" used to try to find solace in the chicken house in the backyard and would use it as a retreat if he recognised storm clouds gathering indoors, but there wasn't always peace, even in the hen run. One old hen made life a misery for the rest and plagued them into a squawking, flapping panic.

They all had bare behinds as a result of her vicious beak. One day their tormentor paid the penalty. "He" caught her by her scraggy neck and pulled it. Even then she did not die kind – she dropped a soft egg all over his slippers. My mother and father thought they were "a couple of tonics" and except for anticipating the amenities of the lean-to, I think they were sorry to see them go.

Our move over the garden wall brought us next door to two real old Victorians. For one of them, the little house had been her childhood home and her companion in retirement joined her there on the death of her parents. They had been friends and workmates at a local cigar factory and at the time we made their acquaintance, they had lived together for many years. They were both spinsters, but there all similarity ended.

One was a replica of the Old Queen's portrait, being small

and dumpy and perpetually dressed in the heavy voluminous black skirts and high-waisted tightly boned bodices of that era. She wore such a collection of undergarments that the old greeny-black barathea skirt beneath its black sateen apron stood away from her waist with crinoline fullness. Thin, silver hair was scraped back from its centre parting into a microscopic bun at the nape of her neck. A round, fresh-complexioned face and pale blue eyes behind old-fashioned steel spectacles belied a stubbornness and determination that rejected all offers of help, however willingly extended or badly needed.

Her companion was just the opposite in appearance, being a thin, worried-looking little woman, though alike in being attired in the inevitable black uniform of the aged. She was, however, in spite of her harassed manner, more talkative and approachable and we liked her better of the two.

They both loved fuchsias and specialised in growing a variety of them in their tiny front garden, which was greatly admired by passers-by when the blooms hung in profusion in summertime. Woe betide us if we were ever caught nipping off a stray bloom which had thrust itself through the wooden-paled fence into our garden. We only had to be caught bending, examining one to bring a rap of knuckles on their windowpane and a pair of steely reprimanding eyes on the other side. If the halfway lacy curtain impeded our prying into their best parlour, it certainly had no detrimental effect on their seeing what went on outside.

Sometimes on a warm day when they opened their front door to sit just inside it enjoying the sight of their fuchsias and watching the world go by, we would run up their garden path and be invited inside. The parlour was papered from the skirting board to the ceiling with dark brown Lincrusta wallpaper, embossed and glossy with years of polishing, so that at a glance it would almost have passed for wooden panelling. For all its shine and serviceableness, it endowed the little room with a depressing heaviness and a feeling of restriction. Even in the summer, with the door flung open to the bright sunshine, it seemed dull to our young eyes and in the wintertime, when only the feeble light of a rainy sky penetrated through the small panes above the lacy curtain, it was dreary beyond words.

If they felt in the right mood and we made ourselves particularly endearing, they brought out a beautiful old musical box from its place in the window recess. Its rosewood case was a glowing tribute to beeswax and turpentine and the hours of loving care which had been bestowed on it were reflected in its unscratched surface. The key was inserted and turned in the slot and liquid notes of the old tunes spilled out into the little room as fresh and tinkling as water drops – fragile reminders of an unhurried past. We loved to listen and to stand and look down through the glass cover, watching the slowly revolving cylinder with its tiny projecting pins.

On several occasions when we accompanied Mother on her visits to them, we were taken through the parlour and into the small living room. It was spotlessly clean and almost monastic in its simplicity of furnishings. There was nowhere to loll. The highly-polished wooden seats of the two small chairs either side of the deal table were cold and hard to our bottoms when we sat on them, legs a-dangle. The black oilcloth covering the scrubbed table-top was bare of plant or flowers. Only the coloured snips in the two hand-made rag rugs which lay on the uneven brick floor, and cushions with cretonne covers, taped to the seats and backs of wooden armchairs either side of the fireplace, softened the otherwise colourless decor. A few pot plants, geraniums and a variegated aspidistra on the window-sill almost touched the bottom of the paper blind which was always drawn down so that only about a third of the tiny squares in the window admitted daylight.

I was always secretly averse to going into that back room, for I dreaded one of the old ladies going to the cupboard by the fireplace with the very mistaken, though understandable, idea that she was going to show us something to delight the heart of a child. Not my heart, though, for the treasure she brought out, lying long and rigid in a cardboard box, always reminded me of the little body, cold in death with its premature teeth. Her box contained a large Victorian doll, its wax face yellowed with age and ghastly in the uncertain light that accentuated the grubby hollows round its painted, staring eyes and prim little mouth. It lay in its shroud of faded lilac silk which had once been a faithful reproduction of a child's party frock. Dusty tufts of hair hung down beneath the large floppy hat, which judging by the remnants of a quill, had once held a curling feather. I loathed it and feared it for its resemblance to my other harrowing experience. Once, she thrust it into my arms; it was heavy, unyielding and smelt damp and fusty, and I disgraced myself and angered my mother by flinging it from me so that it fell with a thud on the snip rug by the fire.

The old ladies' washdays were a revelation to us and often sent us indoors for enlightenment by our mother, for some of the flapping garments on the clothesline mystified us. White linen night caps, frilly-edged with long linen ties, were mistaken by us for cookery caps until mother explained they kept the old ladies' heads and ears warm in their draughty bedrooms. There were red flannel petticoats trimmed with bobbin lace, hand crocheted chemises, flannel nightdresses inflated by the wind into small tents, modesty vests and other weird and wonderful items which set us guessing or giggling. The strangest of all were those which hung almost out of sight by the wall on the far side of their yard – two long legs attached to a waistband, cut so that they overlapped each other at the front and back. These were their 'unmentionables' – Victorian knickers!

Chapter 3

FUN AND GAMES

Mother hated the passageway even more than the privy, for samples of whatever was humped up and down it by the coalmen, the dillymen and others of that ilk, invariably found their way through our side gate and into her living room on our shoes. It was an all-year-round nightmare, but particularly so in the winter months when it became a morass of mud, pock-marked with our marble holes. She bombarded it with ashes almost every day in an effort to stem the tide, but we loved it and spent many happy hours playing there – as my mother put it – "with the rest of the street".

It was an ideal place for playing marbles. The boys rolled theirs along the gutters but we girls liked to thumb ours into a little hole. We loosened the earth first with a piece of stick, dug our shoe heel in and twizzled round until we made a shallow bowl about the diameter of a teacup. More often than not we forgot to change out of our school shoes and presented our poor mother with scuffed toes and filthy heels through twisting in the dirt and kneeling to 'thumby'.

The side wall of the house next door was ideal for one of our favourite ball games and there was ample room for all of us to perform at the same time. The winner was the one who kept her ball bouncing from hand to wall the longest without it dropping, and these eliminating heats often took a considerable time. It says much for the forbearance and even temper of the lady inside the house that she never once came outside to reprimand us for disturbing her peace, yet I had heard for myself the dull thud, thud, thud that our balls made every time they hit against the outside wall of her living room chimney breast. It was a monotonous 'jar' that would have driven my mother to distraction – though not for long! She, however, had a cross to bear as well. We were forever rearranging her ferns and leaving footprints over her flowerbeds in our searches for lost balls.

Sometimes the passageway was a meeting place for a 'pin-a-prick' session. For this game we needed a thick reading book, stiff-covered with a wide spine, and a chance to help ourselves from Mother's postcard album. This was filled with cards of all kinds, some in sets and others sent to her in her courting days which bore sweet words of love from father and made us giggle. I remember one colourful set on the theme of "The Lost Chord"; others were night scenes with frosted embellishments and were very pretty; a lot were stills of the then favourites in the theatre. The idea was to intersperse the picture cards between the pages so that they could not be detected when the book was closed and squeezed tightly. Then a friend, armed with a pin, had to prick the spot where she thought there was a card. If she guessed right, the card became hers; if not, the pin was forfeited and stuck along the spine of the book This game almost always caused dissension between us, especially if the picture pricked was a favourite with the book's owner or if some of the books held postcards of an inferior quality to ours. Great care had to be taken in choosing a book as the leaves had to be of the right consistency – too thin and the pin could not be inserted, too thick and it was a give-away.

If we played in the passageway on Mondays, we kept our eyes and ears alert. About two hundred yards down the street there was a slaughterhouse. Access to it was through two large gates, heavily coated with pitch and riddled with poked-out knotholes. Monday afternoon was always slaughtering day, and pigs, sheep and cows were hung, drawn and quartered there. The arrival of the pigs and sheep was uneventful as they were netted down in horse-drawn floats, but the cows were usually brought on the hoof and as soon as they got within smelling distance of the gates, they went berserk. Often, one would escape the dogs and the flailing arms of the blaspheming drovers, and make a bolt for it – sometimes down our passageway. If we were playing in the backyard when this happened, it was all right. We ran to the wall and had a grandstand view of the bull-running, but if we were in the passageway, it was our turn to run for cover. When all the animals were safely behind the gates, we would rush to the knotholes. I soon found out that "please" would not get me one, so I pushed and jostled with the rest. One very hot summer's day the scrimmage for a knothole was particularly strenuous and I found myself flattened against one of the treacly doors. As I had very long hair, hanging loose, it was asking for trouble. I got stuck. I will draw a veil over my reception when I presented myself at Number 10. Let it suffice to say that for quite a time afterwards I attended school wearing a tammy to hide a very peculiar haircut.

Chapter 4

PUNISHMENT PASTIMES

One day in early February when I was five years old, I came home from school through a heavy snowstorm and found a strange lady in our living room, dishing up the dinner. I could hear Father's voice and Mother's voice in the bedroom above, and then I heard another voice crying – a baby's voice. I rushed upstairs in my snowy boots and there she was, my baby sister, lying warm and pink in the double bed beside mother. I thought she was lovely right from that moment until she could walk, and then I wasn't so sure.

As soon as she could walk she was into everything that was mine, and as soon as she could run she always wanted to go everywhere that I went. While she was too small to lift the latch on the yard gate, I only had to race through and fasten it after me, and she was a prisoner. By the time she had howled her tale of woe to Mother, I was out of sight and free. When she could reach up and open the gate she became my shadow, and I her protesting guardian.

Oh, she was a nuisance! If we played hide and seek she looked through her fingers or else gave the game away. If my marbles took her fancy, especially my multi-coloured glass treasures, I found they were missing from my marble bag

17

hanging behind the door. If I clambered with my friends on to the next-door coalhouse roof and we helped ourselves to fallen pears that lay juicy and yellow on the tiles, she ate her share and then as likely as not, blabbed to mother later in the day. Sometimes though, she got things of mine that she didn't want, like whooping cough and my cut-down frocks. When she was old enough to accompany me when I went with friends to The Pictures, she invariably wanted to spend a penny just as the lights began to dim, even though we had been sitting for ages waiting impatiently for that very moment. Until she could read for herself, I had to gabble the sense of every one of the printed captions which came on the screen between action shots, or else she wanted to know "What are they saying?" and "Why are they doing that?", incessantly.

She wore my patience thin on many occasions and did not always get away with just being shouted at. If I lost my temper and meted out corporal punishment, her mouth became a big, round 'O' and her voice preceded her all the way home, so that Mother was alerted long before we arrived and sometimes she would come out to investigate before I could make myself scarce. When this happened I was usually bundled back through the gate and unless I could make myself heard above the din of the wronged and justify my actions, I was sent up to bed for an hour or two.

As time went on she became less dependent upon me and acquired friends of her own age, and I gained more freedom to come and go with mine. Our squabbles outside the gate became less frequent but we still crossed swords on home ground, usually over possessions. This jangling brought

Mother hot-foot to arbitrate, or to warn us, if arbitration was unworkable, that we should both get what we deserved if we brought her back again. We had good reason to know she was a woman of her word, but all the same we sometimes thought our rights were worth defending and paid the penalty with smarting bottoms.

There were times when we dispensed with words altogether and there was a pitched battle with, in my sister's case, no holds barred. She fought for her life with feet, fists and on one occasion her teeth, and more often than not she won. These battles brought us into real disgrace. Mother opened the staircase door, and in a tone that allowed for no argument, told us to go to bed and Father would deal with us when he came home. We marched up in single file with sullen faces, and perhaps got in a last backward kick or sudden push in the dark, then sat with backs to one another on either side of the bed, in silence.

Eventually we would hear Father's voice in conversation with Mother downstairs and after a while, the staircase door being opened and his feet ascending. Usually he left the house long before we were awake, and travelled too far to come home again until the early evening, so that we were always eager to see him and invariably, when he pushed open the bedroom door we forgot our disgrace and jumped off the bed to welcome him. What could he do to the owners of arms that hugged him and faces that smiled into his? Mother was downstairs with an ear cocked for his reprimand, so disentangling himself, he sat between us on the bed and in a suitably loud and solemn voice, 'read the riot act' to us and then left us to repent until Mother thought fit to shout us down again.

Sometimes his homecoming was delayed and our waiting time in the bedroom became so prolonged that we buried the hatchet and snuggled down together for a read. He would come into the bedroom later and find the culprits lying amidst a litter of comics, fast asleep. At other times, when we had exhausted all the bedside reading and were bored with sitting around, we looked for something else to pass the time. Usually, our eyes went to the tin trunk which stood in a corner of the room, beneath a starched coverlet. Mother used it for storing bed linen, out-of-season clothing and other odds and ends. We raised its lid and emptied it and repacked it more than once, unbeknown to her, and around Christmas time, we found things in there that made our eyes sparkle and our tongues itch to betray our knowledge.

Once we had a lovely time whilst awaiting Father's lecture. The large double bed we shared was covered with a counterpane which had thick, deep fringing all round its valance. It, and its twin in her bedroom, were Mother's pride and joy and we had been warned not to spill things on it or mark it with our boots. It was a showpiece, and when bedtime came it was turned back in neat folds to lie across the foot of the bed, revealing a warm patchwork quilt. On this day of our disgrace, one of us had a brainwave: "Let's plait the fringe!"

We started the joyous pastime on opposite sides of the bed and did not meet at the bottom until over an hour later. By that time we had plaited dozens and dozens of tight little pigtails. Our fingers were stiff and aching and our cheeks burned with the concentrated effort. We stood back to admire our handiwork and were well pleased. It was a wonderful achievement and we were disappointed that Father never noticed anything different when he came upstairs to us. We certainly did not anticipate the effect it would have on Mother when bedtime came.

We followed her upstairs and waited just inside the door until she crossed the room in the dark and put a match to the gas bracket over the bedhead and drew the curtains across the window. We watched her turn and bend over the bed to fold back the counterpane. Then we saw her freeze with astonishment and disbelief at what she saw. The storm broke over us. Father heard it and came bounding up to see whatever could have caused it, when only minutes before he had said goodnight to two young daughters who were the best of friends with Mother. When she pointed to the rows of little pigtails, he looked across at our two guilty faces and we saw mirth in his eyes and a twitch on his lips. To Mother's chagrin, he laughed and laughed until the tears ran down his face. We knew better than to join in, though we felt glad he had diverted Mother's fury from us for the time being, and we took advantage of it and leapt into bed. The next morning we tried, with Mother, to unravel the plaits, but the strands were hard to separate and when teased with a comb, turned into fuzz instead of hanging straight. In the end they had to be cut off and the raw edges hemmed and disguised with bobble braid.

Our bedroom banishments did not occur very frequently, for although we squabbled, we did not often come to blows, nor were we ever subjected to more than a smack on our bottoms when really naughty. Even then, it was never Father's hand that descended. A word of reproach from him was always enough to shame us to tears. Greed, cheek and telling tales were the things that got us into trouble and we soon learned that these vices were unacceptable from "nice little girls".

Only once do I remember Father really storming into our bedroom, and on this occasion we had not been sent there because of naughtiness. It happened one Sunday afternoon in high summer when the windows were flung wide to entice in any breeze, and the curtains were drawn against the intense heat. Sunday School had been suspended for a few weeks because of the holiday season, and so we were at home and at a loose end. Father, as was his custom after dinner on Sundays, had gone to stretch out for half an hour in the other bedroom and Mother was having 'five minutes with the paper' in an armchair downstairs. All was peaceful and quiet, too much so for us, and we decided to liven things up a bit with a little music.

Some weeks previously an aunt whom we seldom saw, remembered us when she wanted to get rid of an ancient clockwork gramophone, and she sent word to Mother that it had been despatched to us by rail. It eventually arrived and was handed in at our front door by the drayman, together with its huge, green fluted horn. There was also a separate parcel containing about a dozen records and a box of needles.

We were delighted with it and regaled Mother and Father with its tinny renderings of "Pretty Polly Perkins", "Who were you with last night'?" and other favourites. The one we enjoyed most was a tenor rendering of "Men of Harlech". It had a crack across the record which caused the needle to stick and our tenor repeated "Men of Harlech ... of Harlech ... of Harlech .... of Harlech", ad infinitum. If the gramophone spring was fully wound he sang fast and high, but of course, as it ran down, so did he, slurring his words and going off-key to a deep, slow rumbling bass, at which point we revved him up again without lifting the needle and sent him scurrying back up the scale as if he had been pricked. We thought he was a scream and made our knickers damp with laughing at him.

He was our natural choice on this flat Sunday afternoon and, as usual, we wound him up and let him run down, time and time again, and rolled about on the bed convulsed with laughter, quite oblivious to his effect upon the neighbours and with never a thought for two sleeping parents. His effect on one of them was catastrophic for him, and us. We never heard the ping of the bedsprings in the next room, nor the pad of feet, but there stood Father! He wrested the gramophone from the chair seat. Our tenor gave a last strangled "Men of Haaaaaa ..." as the pick-up slithered across the still spinning record, and that was the last time we ever heard him.

When I went outside the next morning to empty a bowl for Mother, I found "Men of Harlech" in two pieces in the dustbin.

Chapter 5

THE PICTURES

We looked forward to Saturday afternoons. It was mat-
inée day at the Scala Picture House, when we renewed
our adventures with Pearl White, Harold Lloyd, Charlie
Chaplin, Rin Tin Tin, Thelma Todd and Patsy Kelly, and
other 'greats' of the silent screen. How we loved them all.

Mother gave us twopence each and Father felt in his pocket and handed each of us a penny to spend. Sometimes we
made a slight detour and paid a visit to an old sugar-boiler.
We loved the smells of aniseed, clove, peppermint and pear
drops which wafted through his open door. We crowded into
his little room with our friends, and peeped into the shining
vats with their bubbling mess of sweets-to-come. He would
give us half a pound of broken pieces for a halfpenny, all
cane sugar and delicious, and off we would run, with still a
halfpenny left to spend.

The Scala was situated in the Market Place, and although
Wednesday was the official market day, there were always a
lot of stalls on a Saturday afternoon. Right outside the
Picture House was a fruit and nut stall, whose till was soon
full with the halfpennies and pennies we all sacrificed for
bags of monkey nuts in their shells.

The main entrance to the Picture House was very grand
with a black and white tiled floor and trailing plants ranged
along each side as one walked through. Our entrance was
vastly different. It was down a narrow passage and at the
far end, set high in the wall, was a window. This was our goal
and we joined the jostling queue of happy children until the
'lady' deigned to open it for business. I never grew tall
enough to see her, and when it was my turn I held up our
twopences and received pieces of metal shaped like
swastikas, with a hole in the centre. These were our pass-
ports to heaven for an hour or two, and we held them tightly until we reached the old superintendent who stood guard
at the rear entrance. He counted our heads as he collected
the disks to thread on to a long steel rod at his side – and
then we were in!

Those who were 'in arms' went in free. I think the old man
must have had a kind heart or extremely bad eyesight, for
some of the free customers were almost the size of the car-
riers, and I am sure he often had a job to see who was carrying who.

Our seats were always very near the front, and whilst we
had a close-up of all that went on, we also had cricked necks
and had to tolerate the rainy effect of the old, silent films.
Bedlam reigned while we waited for the lights to go out and
the orchestra to assemble in the pit a few yards from where
we sat. Everyone ate, shouted to friends, swapped seats,
spent a quick penny, and generally enjoyed themselves. If
the orchestra seemed to be dallying, they sometimes
received a shower of monkey nut shells or orange peel to
spur them on. If somebody big impeded the view and refused

to change places, there was sometimes a fight, which the old man quelled by threatening to evict both sides. The victor rarely enjoyed his triumph because the vanquished either pinched his bottom or kicked his seat underneath during the performance.

We laughed and shouted and sometimes cried, and read the captions to those amongst us who could not read.

Rin Tin Tin, the Alsatian dog, was everybody's favourite, but he was a tear-jerker for he usually starved, got lost or escaped death by inches, and on these occasions, we were generally standing up already, with excitement or anxiety, when the lights came on for "The King".

If we could evade the vigilant eyes of the old man, we liked to slip underneath the red barrier cords looped across the aisles, and mingle with our 'betters' as they filed out between the potted plants. We had no ideas of snobbery in doing this; we were all far too near the earth to know what that meant, but it was perhaps a delaying tactic to prolong the atmosphere of the film or maybe just nosiness.

The impact of daylight and the raucous voices of the stall-holders outside would rouse us from our celluloid trance. We remembered we were hungry and ran home, hoping for some treat for tea.

Chapter 6

DRAINS AND RIVERS

When we talked to our north country cousins about going to the Drains to fish, they looked askance at us, for they associated the word with waste-pipes and street grids. All lovers of the Fens know them, not only for keeping the rich, fertile land – much of it below sea level and reclaimed from the sea – free from flood water in wintertime, but for fishing, boating, skating and bird-life. We loved them for the beauty of the wild flowers and grasses which grew in such profusion on their banks.

My father was an all-the-year-round angler, fishing in fresh water and tidal. I often went with him, first as a passenger on his crossbar and later on a bicycle of my own. He fished the fens for miles around and I can still remember some of the lovely names of those we visited – Hob Hole, Mount Pleasant, Cowbit and Cherry Corner. Sometimes we inspected several stretches before he found water of the right colour, not too clear and not too reedy. Whilst he settled down on his wicker basket to assemble his tackle, opening the tin of gentles and soaking the bread ready to throw around the float to attract the fish, I went exploring.

Every season had its attractions. The trees and bushes

were alive with busy birds in springtime and a glory in May
when they were in blossom. The grassy banks were confet-
tied with wild flowers the summer through. Grasses grew
until they were waist high and I hunted for my favourite,
the lovely quaking grass which we children called 'tottie'
grass.

I lay on my stomach and parted the roots to watch the
antics of beetles and colonies of ants, and sometimes star-
tled a grasshopper or disturbed a bumblebee. Once I felt a
movement beneath my hand and was astonished and frightened when a grass snake emerged, as scared as I was, and
glided through the grass into the water.

I kept well away from my father's cast and learned not to
make a lot of movement or noise around him. If I became at
all fidgety he would delve into his basket and find a comic
for me to read, and either an apple or piece of chocolate to
keep me happy. Sometimes when the fish were slow to bite,
he would leave the rod and explore with me. He was a country boy and through him I learned much of the ways of bird
and beast.

I loved to accompany him from early autumn onwards,
when the trees and bushes were ready for harvesting. My
mother sometimes came too at this time, and we gathered
the bluish-purple sloes that looked so ripe and tasted so bitter. We knew where there were crab apples for making jelly,
and of course, we made more than one excursion to pick
blackberries.

The 'Sheffielders' knew our Drains too and descended
upon us by the trainload in summertime. Horse-drawn wagonettes awaited them at the station or in the Market Place

and they clambered in with their tackle to be taken along the country roads to the favourite fishing spots. They lined the banks of the Drains on both sides, especially on Sundays when special train excursions were run for their benefit. Many of them were crippled or disfigured through injury in the mines or steel works and we felt glad they could come away from the smoke and dirt for a few hours.

The two rivers, one tidal and the other fresh water, which came to town and shouted at each other through the sluice gates, leave very different memories. The first threaded its way to the North Sea, washing the mudflats, filling the creeks and seeping up beneath the sea pinks and over the saltings. It bore the merchantmen to discharge their cargoes at the dock and eddied around the fishing smacks as they tacked from side to side to trap the wind in their sails. It divided to fill the dock basin and then raced past cranes, under the swing bridge and behind the shops and parish church, to be thwarted at last by the sluice gates, just beyond.

Its freshwater neighbour on the other side had wandered some 30 placid miles between fertile fields and gentle banks. It watered wading cattle, rocked the small river craft anchored in its shallows and jostled the rowing boats tethered together on either side of the boathouse. It was the venue for rowing clubs and we blistered our hands, struggling to keep the oars in the rowlocks and steer a straight course along it. Although it did the same essential job as the humble Drains, it was definitely a more snooty relation. People strolled alongside it during summer evenings or sat primly upon seats beneath the trees on hot Sunday afternoons.

Chapter 7

GOING DOWN BELOW

Going 'Down Below', I thank providence, was a misnomer for a glorious day out in a large dinghy on the tidal river. The sailing party usually numbered about twenty, mostly mothers with their children, though occasionally there would be a sprinkling of fathers and big brothers. Weather permitting, these trips were always undertaken on Sundays throughout the summer, whenever tides were right for the journey both ways.

Our captain and his mate were man and wife, and as I remember them, in their sixties. They were a wonderful old couple. She was buxom in her navy serge skirt and white blouse with its sleeves rolled up above her elbows, busy seating each arriving party in the boat. She stowed away the primus stoves, rearranged tarpaulins to make room for oil cans and the flagons of fresh water, and generally saw that everyone was comfortable, ready for casting off. He would be up on the quayside, a tanned muscular figure in his thigh waders and fisherman's jersey, waiting to steady us down the steep stone steps and into the boat. His hair was still brown and clung to his head like a curly cap, framing ears which were pierced with gold 'sleepers'. In his younger days he had been a skipper on one of the fishing smacks, and like the majority of sailors in little ships which depended on wind and sail, he had a deep reverence for his Maker and a respect for the river he knew so well.

Word would come to my mother that a trip was on, and we would count the days to Sunday. She baked on Saturday and packed everything in readiness – food in plenty, for the strong air made us ravenous – tea and sugar in paper 'screws', a bottle of fresh water, lugless cups or the tops of flasks which had come to grief, and fresh milk. There were old sandshoes for us to paddle in and protect our feet when we scrambled about the boulders looking for winkles, and woollies in case it turned cold on the homeward journey. She also packed towels and a change of clothes, in anticipation of us falling in or getting so covered in mud as to be unpresentable for the walk through town on the Sunday evening. Our disembarkation often coincided with the exodus of churchgoers from evening service at the parish church, which towered above us in all its magnificence as we climbed with our baggage onto the quay.

The boat was bobbing on the swell, straining at the thick twist of rope which looped through an iron ring in the Doughty Quay wall. We found some of our friends already seated and once we had been helped in amidst cries of "Be careful!" or "Mind the cans!", we knew we could look forward to a wonderful day.

The journey took several hours as the river wound some nine miles between the seabanks before we reached Down Below, and the old couple, each with a pair of strong oars, rowed, rested and rowed again. On both the outward and homeward journeys we went with the tide. It would be on the turn when we embarked and we came home as it was coming in, so that the rowers gained considerable impetus from the fast-flowing current in both directions. Nevertheless, it was no mean feat of endurance, especially on the homeward trip when the water came almost up to the rowlocks with the added load of samphire, cockles and mussels that we had all gathered during the day and stowed away beneath the seats and between our legs. Our journey from the quay and down river was full of excitement. We waved to all who stood and stared as we passed by; we craned our necks as we threaded between the huge pillars of the swing bridge and saw the cranes at work in the dock and along the timber wharves. We stood up to point at the ships we could glimpse between the dock buildings as we sidled past on the far side and headed between the mudflats and the grey-green saltings. When the sun shone, it made jewels of the water drops which cascaded from the oars as they rose and fell.

The day was ours and we sang and pointed to things that caught our eyes as we went along. We knelt on the wooden seats to look into the water and sometimes were rewarded by the sight of hundreds of jellyfish, rising and falling just below the surface, so that their translucent bodies glowed with rainbow colours. Gulls dipped and called to us and sometimes rode the waves alongside, waiting for us to throw a crust. Cows, grazing in isolation on the top of grassy banks, lifted their heads at the noisy boatload of children going by.

Our biggest thrill was to meet a 'big ship', usually Swedish or Norwegian, on its way to the dock to off-load a cargo of timber. I think most of us were a little afraid when we saw it bearing down upon us, for we were dwarfed by its high sloping side as it slid by. Our guardians would row us into the side of the river so that we were as far away as possible from the draw of the ship as it came close, to avoid pitching and tossing in its wake. There would be an exchange of shouted greetings between members of its crew and our captain, and much laughing and waving on both sides. Sometimes the music of a mouth organ or accordion would waft down to us from the deck, and once a hand of bananas was lowered in an old basket and retrieved by our captain with a boathook.

When we rounded the final bend in the river, there before us was Down Below. We could see the end of the seabanks, the end of the saltings, and standing at the river mouth was the lighthouse. Beyond it, the open sea – the Deeps – and in the distance, riding at anchor, the pilot sloop.

Our captain would veer to the right-hand side of the river and scan the water's edge until he found a safe place for us to land. We hurriedly gathered bags and baskets together and changed into our old shoes. He and his wife helped us to find a safe footing between the glistening, sea-weeded boulders, and we made our way up the grassy slope at the bank's end. His wife would join us with the stoves and water flagons, while he climbed back into the boat and rowed it round the headland to beach it safely. We children were agog to get busy with our buckets and spades and to paddle at the water's edge which shone and rippled far below us. As the tide receded we had a great expanse of hard, crimpy sand to play on in absolute safely. We were free to romp and splash about, stripped down to an old vest and knickers.

The grown-ups flung themselves on the level top of the bank until tea was brewed on the primus stoves. Later on, some of them scrambled down to join us, and we went back to the boulders to hunt for winkles which hung on their slimy undersides. The foot of the lighthouse yielded the largest and was a favourite hunting ground. Then we wandered farther afield to where we could see the sturdy samphire plants. These we gathered and tied into bundles, washing the sand from their roots before putting them into bags. In the far distance, a black shadow stretched across the skyline – it was the mussel beds. These too we raided and added to the store of cockles which we had so diligently searched for and dug from their hidey-holes beneath the sand.

The sun came to rest on the water ahead of us as we joined the fishing smacks on the homeward journey. Once back at Number 10, mother fetched the zinc bath from its nail on the wall outside, filled it from the little boiler and washed us down. There were no 'kneeling prayers' that night, we were so tired we said them in bed and hoped God wouldn't mind.

Chapter 8

SCHOOLDAYS

Ours was an infant, middle and senior school, all rolled into one, with boys and girls mingled from the age of five to fourteen. Nobody thought the arrangement at all odd, or asking for trouble. It was the order of the day, and order was enforced whether the teacher was a man or a woman. We behaved or we were caned.

School was about two minutes' run from home for me and about twenty minutes' pull-and-push for my poor mother when my sister started. She didn't like it and she wasn't going. It took a very long time and many a battle before she was finally convinced she had no choice.

The school buildings were pleasant and set back from the road behind a lawn, complete with flagpole. There were separate entrances for boys and girls and they were segregated again at playtime into two spacious playgrounds, and at the far end of these was a plot of ground for the boys to garden.

We were enrolled when we were five and spent the next nine years in more or less the same company of teachers and classmates, moving up room by room through the years, until we became school-leavers. Our work and characters were encouraged and we escaped the readjustment that is necessary when children transfer from school to school in various age groups.

Our classrooms were airy and well-windowed, and housed thirty to forty children. There was no central heating, but I remember with pleasure the enormous coal fires behind protective iron fireguards. Woe betide anyone caught leaning against or sitting on these. I did so one summer when the grate was empty and lost my balance. I did a backward somersault and gave everyone around an eyeful of my white knee-length knickers with their broderie anglaise frills.

We met winters in a woollen vest, combinations which were top to bottom monstrosities with flaps, fleecy-lined liberty bodice, knickers, one flannelette underskirt, one lightweight underskirt, a serge frock with long sleeves, a pinny, and usually a hand-knitted cardigan, long black stockings held up with elastic garters and either buttoned or laced boots. Central heating would have killed us!

If colds were rife in the school, we were safeguarded with a small cotton bag enclosing a square of camphor, hung around our necks on a length of tape. Besides keeping us warm, the liberty bodices were there to anchor our knickers, for nobody had heard of bloomers with elastic. As well as their front button fastening, there was a button on each side seam and another on the centre back. These matched the buttonholes in the top band of our knickers, and it was essential that we should learn to button up the front flap first, otherwise there was the possibility that we might do something in haste, and repent at leisure.

The pinny was usually made of white cambric or fine linen, with a yoke and epaulettes of broderie anglaise or lace insertion, and when new, often boasted a piece of ribbon threaded through the yoke. This adornment usually lasted until the first wash and then became a hair ribbon. The pinny was well starched before ironing, so that the epaulettes stood up stiffly on top of our shoulders and the tape fastening ruched the material round our necks so that we winced every time we turned our heads.

A few of the boys who had old-fashioned mothers presented themselves in suits with sailor collars. Celluloid collars were regular wear and so were cloth caps with covered cardboard peaks which fastened to the crown with a large press stud. After being kicked about the cloakroom and a few soakings in the rain, the cardboard went to pulp inside the cloth and the peak relied upon the press stud to save it from falling over the wearer's face. Country boys came in winter wearing brown corduroy suits with knee breeches that exuded an odour like wet rags which had been folded up and forgotten.

It was a church school and our days began and ended with assembly in the Hall for prayers and a hymn, followed in the mornings by a dossier of our misdemeanours and the punishments to be meted out.

There was no time spent on organised games; schooltime was for learning, and any recreation apart from physical exercise in the playground once or twice a week, was indulged in at playtime or after four o'clock. Football, swimming and netball were popular with us, but there were no refinements. The boys had a football and that was all. The goal was a pile of their clothes at each end of the pitch and they played in ordinary boots. We wore distinguishing tapes pinned to our shoulders in the netball games, to save chaos, and we had proper goalposts, but we too played in our everyday clothes, though some of us managed to persuade our mothers to buy us a pair of sandshoes. Our artistic talent was encouraged with coloured wax crayons, chalks and brown paper, though later on we produced quite creditable results in charcoal and watercolours. Music lessons were a torture as they were presided over by the Headmaster himself. We warbled up and down the scale, time and time again, before he was satisfied or became too disgusted to care.

Sewing lessons in the junior classrooms always confined themselves to seams, gussets and tucks, or specimen darning; preparatory exercises for making up the piles of already cut out knickers, underskirts, aprons and so on, which awaited us the following year on the shelves in the senior sewing room. The monotony was broken for us on one occasion, when we received a special consignment of long, white cotton shifts. These were brought to us by one of the ladies on the Board of Governors whose missionary sister intended to distribute them to her converts in the African bush. Her instructions were that we must sew them strongly and put in ample gussets because they loved to dance so strenuously.

We never met crinolined ladies waiting to come to life in coloured silks, or presented our mother with a set of fancy-worked tray-cloths. She was the recipient of indifferently knitted string dishcloths during our initiation period with the knitting needles, while socks, scarves and gloves were the most exciting things that hung from them later on, when we became more proficient.

Nevertheless, we were thoroughly trained in the three Rs. Arithmetic tables became as familiar to us as our own handwriting, through repetitive recitation and copying down. Handwriting developed flow and neatness as a result of our careful emulation of copperplate specimens. We learned to read with 'expression' and identify unfamiliar words by building them up phonetically, and in due time, a fair proportion of us made the grade to grammar school.

We knew our place in the presence of our elders and grew up reasonably happy and contented with our lot. We were encouraged to save and every Monday morning saw us in a queue before the teacher's desk, waiting to invest anything from a penny up to sixpence. The penny was by far the most popular coin, and we rarely held more in our hands, except on birthdays or some very special occasion.

Chapter 9

COOKERY CAPERS

After attending school to qualify for our attendance mark and to pay in our bank money on Monday mornings, we older girls were trusted to make our way, unchaperoned, to the church hall for cookery lessons. It was quite a distance from the school and we took our time. We often saw the cookery mistress when we turned the last corner, standing on the pavement watch in hand, waiting for us.

The hall was an ugly building, standing in a paved yard behind iron railings, and enclosed on either side by crumbling brick walls. It was a real eyesore to the residents of the large houses which surrounded it, for the road was residential and select. The church was on the same side of the road, a few hundred yards further on, but hidden from the hall by a bend in the road. The hall was just as depressing inside. There was staging at one end and although it was a spacious room, the windows along its length were high, dirty and faced the blank side walls of nearby houses, so that daylight was restricted and the gas brackets were alight more often than not

We worked in pairs at long trestle tables and shared utensils and cutlery. Those of us with more trusting mothers

brought our own ingredients, but the rest used those provided for them and had the option of buying the finished
dish at the end of each session.

We hacked, chopped or minced, and weighed, mixed and
tasted, and finally jostled together in front of the giant stove
in the far corner of the room to place our *pièces de resistance*
in one of the cavernous ovens. Boiled puddings, stews or
soups bubbled or simmered in large, two-handled containers
on the hotplates and bread, buns and small cakes filled the
two ovens on either side of the coal fire.

When preparation was completed and while cooking was
taking place, we opened our recipe books and carefully wrote
our list of ingredients and procedure. Sometime during the
morning, depending on the intricacy of the menu, we had a
short playtime in the confines of the paved yard.

As most of us had long hair, either hanging loose or in pigtails, we had to encase it in frilly-edged mob caps, and unless
it was the day for cleaning the flues or utensils – on which
occasions we wore hessian aprons – we had coarse, linen
pinafores and white armlets from wrist to elbow.

One Monday morning there was to be a society wedding at
the church. A daughter of one of the town's dignitaries was
to marry a high-ranking officer in the Royal Air Force. He
was so 'high' that there was to be a fly-past of aircraft over
the church as the couple emerged and we decided amongst
ourselves that if the opportunity presented itself, we would
attend.

Luck was with us, for the preceding week we were told to
bring the ingredients for steak and kidney pudding, which is
not a very long or involved job to prepare and tie up in its

basin, ready for the pot. We all worked with a will that must have surprised our instructress. When all the basins were submerged up to their rims in boiling water, we were told we could go into the forecourt to play. We allowed a few minutes to elapse, sufficient to give her time to go into the caretaker's house at the rear of the hall for her usual cup of tea and gossip. Then we hurried up the road to the church, still attired in mob caps, aprons and armlets.

The last of the guests, elegant in furs, morning-dress and uniforms, were filing into the church when we arrived. There were raised eyebrows amongst the knot of gawpers around the gate as we brushed past them and in two-by-two formation, went up the winding path to the church porch. The young ushers saw us coming and from their bewildered looks, must have thought at first that we were an outsize contingent of bridesmaids. As we had our heads covered, we knew we could enter the church without interference, so when one of the young men asked us "Which side?", somebody said "Friends of the bride", and we shuffled after him and sat ourselves in the two rear pews. I believe our entrance caused almost as much sensation as the bride's, but no-one had the courage to come and evict us, so we saw everything. It was a lovely wedding, but we dare not stop while the newlyweds signed the register, so we tiptoed out. Once clear of the porch we ran back to the puddings, but as we rounded the bend, we knew our luck had deserted us. Our cookery mistress and the caretaker's wife were out in the road looking for us. We were lectured on the enormity of our escapade and it did not help matters when we lifted the lids off the cooking pots and saw string, soggy greaseproof paper and several empty basins swirling round in porridgy water.

We had a very good friend who often swallowed the evidence of our cookery failures. He was the dachshund who lived in a house beside the hall. He knew Monday mornings as well as we did, and would rush out, barking as soon as he heard us in the forecourt. He devoured many a rock cake and 'sad' pastry that we lobbed over to him and became so fat that his body almost touched the ground. In the end, our secret leaked out when his owner explained to our cookery mistress that our kindness was doing him bodily harm.

Chapter 10

EMPIRE DAY

Although Victoria, Queen of the United Kingdom of Great Britain and Ireland and Empress of India, had been dead for more than twenty years, her birthday on May 24th was an important date in our calendar. It was Empire Day – a school holiday and a day of celebration.

We were all familiar with her stern profile and that of her bearded son, King Edward VII, for they were on many of the pennies that we handled. We heard, and believed, that so widespread was her Empire, that the sun could never set upon it and we sang with fervour, "Rule Britannia!"

Our headmaster brought out the big Union Jack from its cupboard and prepared it for hoisting to the top of the flag-pole on the morning of the great day. We queued around our teacher's desk a few days beforehand to receive a coloured ticket for presentation at the tea tent and several white ones to be surrendered for free rides on the roundabouts and swings, together with a detailed programme of events and clear instructions of the part we were to play in them. All these we gave to our mother for safe-keeping.

She blancoed our canvas shoes, looked out our white knee length socks and hung our best summer dresses on hangers behind the bedroom door. Clean handkerchiefs were folded into pockets in our knickers, new satin hair ribbons were bought and shaped pieces cut out of the ends to stop them fraying. The occasion was important enough to warrant new dresses sometimes, if those we had were still too short for decency after being let down, for many eyes would be upon us. Our hair was washed and wound into 'rags' and off we went to bed, praying for a fine day. We would wake to a lovely summer morning, 'Victoria's weather', for it was said that her great occasions were always blessed with sunshine.

Our skipping and jumping around Mother in the tiny living room drove her to give us an early dinner, array us in all our finery and wave us goodbye. We called for our friends and then made our way to the Market Place, to congregate with the rest of our schoolmates behind the large banner with the name of our school printed on it. Each school had its own standard bearer and soon there was a seething mass of happy, chattering children, dressed in their Sunday best. Teachers kept us in order before we moved off to the music of the Town Band. We each had a flag to carry as we marched in procession between the long lines of sightseers. It must have been a sight, for there were hundreds of children, all in summery clothes, waving Union Jacks and singing. The route led from the Market Place, through the town centre past beflagged shops, to New Park. The wrought iron gates were open to receive us, and as we followed behind the Band, each child received an orange and a packet of sweets. The crowd pressed in at the end of our procession and the rest of the day was ours to enjoy as we liked. The park was full of entertainment, people and noise.

Swings, coconut shies and sideshows all vied for our patronage. The balloon man and toffee apple vendors pushed temptation under our noses and soon wheedled the pennies out of our pockets. The Rock King with his waxed moustache and stetson stood behind his stall with its piled-up rock, gingerbread and brandy-snaps, serving as fast as he could and throwing the money into a galvanized bucket near his elbow. Punch and Judy caused a bottleneck near the ambulance tent and kept us enthralled. We wandered around enjoying ourselves, and keeping a lookout for our mother.

A freshly mown area of grass had been railed off for interschool sports and we sat with our friends and groaned or cheered as we watched our school gladiators pit their strength against the rest of the field. Then we shuffled into the tea tent with its smell of tea and cake and bruised grass, and sat at long trestle tables.

Fathers went home to a lonely tea, spruced themselves up and joined mothers in the early evening, when the tug-of-war and greasy pole were the main attractions. The latter was a real spectacular and caused much laughter and great disappointment to the unfortunate slitherers who scrabbled and climbed in vain. Then someone would come along and reap the advantage of the surplus grease being already rubbed off onto the clothes of his predecessors, and slowly climbing, and slipping and climbing again, would reach the top. A great cheer would go up as he unfastened the prize voucher and waved it ecstatically in acknowledgement.

Gradually, the sun went down and the dew began to fall. We saw the snaky fingers of a heat mist curling between the trees, and tiny white moths beginning to stir among the evergreen bushes at the back of the flowerbeds. The crowds thinned and Mother said it was time for us to go. We didn't mind, it had been a long, happy day.

Chapter 11

SUNDAY SCHOOL

Almost everyone we knew attended morning and afternoon at Sunday School, except the rebels who started out and then played truant, or the downright unruly who flatly refused to go. My sister was one of these, and remembering the tussle to get her to day school, my mother gave in.

I attended classes in the church hall, but it had one great disadvantage; our headmaster lived on the opposite side of the road and in fine weather he saw far too much for our good on Sunday mornings. As the boys put it, he was 'always mucking about' behind the garden hedge and had a grandstand view of horseplay and other prankish behaviour that went on while we waited for someone to unlock the hall door. We presented our card to the superintendent as we entered and he stamped another attendance star on it. Without sufficient of these, our prizes were in jeopardy and we stood a chance of being rejected when the school treat came along.

The floor space in the hall was shared by several classes at the same time. Teachers made a square with the wooden forms we used at our cookery classes, and sat in the centre on a chair. Small texts were distributed each Sunday and we kept these safely at home until we had six to show to our teacher. Then we received a much larger text to hang on our bedroom wall, usually embellished with a wreath of flowers encircling a warning such as "The Wages of Sin is Death".

After receiving our attendance star in the afternoon, we walked in line to church for the children's service. The vicar left his pulpit and talked to us in his gentle, scholarly voice about the baby Jesus and the infant Moses or the leper and the blind man. He chose hymns he knew we could sing and understand: "We are but little children weak" and "All things bright and beautiful". He, himself, was a friend of little children and we loved him. Summertime brought our Sunday School Treat and as we were only some twenty-five miles from the coast, we went to Skegness for the day. It really was a treat, for opportunity and money rarely came together in any of our families to enable them to take us on such excursions. We assembled with our mothers in the early morning, encumbered with the usual bags of food, towels and other crisis gear which were deemed necessary for a day out.

We shaded our eyes and peered up the road to the distant bridge which spanned the Drain, willing the convoy of open-topped buses to arrive. When they did, there was a rush by the boys and tomboys for the staircases to the upper decks, while the young, old and timid settled themselves downstairs. The road was full of bends and the old buses, with their small wheels and solid tyres, swayed and rolled round them all. We were pitched and tossed so that there were some among us who looked green before we had gone many miles on the journey. These indispositions were easily dealt with. There was very little traffic and we only had to whisper to our teacher and she, or our vicar, tapped a distress signal on the glass partition, and the driver would come to a halt on a wide grass verge. He then waited patiently while we went behind the hedge or into a dyke to relieve our feelings, in one way or another.

Where trees overhung the road, a game of touch went on behind the backs of the teachers on the top deck, to see who could grasp a branch as the bus passed underneath. One or two of the company narrowly missed being airborne through being unable to let go quickly enough, but we all survived to reach journey's end. We were hurried past the tantalising shops along the main street and down to the seafront where there was little else but sand dunes, the sea and the donkeys. Our mothers knew that apart from a donkey ride, a stick of rock to take home, or perhaps a halfpenny cornet from the hokey-pokey man, we would be content to paddle and play until teatime.

Tea of sandwiches, jellies and cake was prepared for us in a first floor room above a confectionery shop, and we did justice to it after a day in the open air.

An anticlimax usually set in on the homeward journey, and one or two of the outside riders sneaked inside the bus for warmth. The rest sat close and turned up coat collars. Somebody began to sing, but few had enough energy to join him and he fell silent. We paid scant attention to the view, except to estimate how many more miles we still had to travel.

Father was usually at the other end to meet us, and relieved our weary legs by giving each of us, in turn, piggy backs all the way home.

Chapter 12

BATHING BELLES

In our environment, it was only common sense to encourage children to learn to swim. The town was divided by a drain and two rivers, and the surrounding countryside was a network of waterways. We could not escape water and in was inevitable that we should fall in sometime on our rambles, though Mother always warned us to keep well away from the banks.

Learning to swim and save lives was part of our school curriculum and several times a week during summer term, we were allowed out of school early to go along to the Corporation swimming baths. It was a long and devious route, and as we had barely half an hour allotted to us for the lesson when we arrived, including undressing in the cubicles, we had to think up ways to make the most of our time in the water. It became imperative to don bathing costumes underneath our clothes sometime during the afternoon, and discard as much underwear as decency would allow and roll it into a towel. Playtime was our first chance and as soon as the bell sounded, we raced into the playground and made a smart capture of an empty lavatory. The difficulty was to keep it for long. We had to struggle with so many buttons, tapes and layers, that before the striptease was completed, there were hammerings and kickings and threats to tell teacher. Others further along were similarly occupied behind closed doors, so legitimate use of the half a dozen lavatories was temporarily suspended. As playtime was limited and no one was 'excused' afterwards, those in dire need were both worried and angry. The time came, as it was bound to come, when somebody had an accident and to save face and a telling-off, blurted out the reason to the teacher. That sabotaged future time-saving. Perhaps it was just as well, for we used to run the whole way, half-clothed, and arrived with faces the colour of beetroot and beaded with perspiration. The superintendent looked at us and led us into a side room to cool off, so we gained nothing in the end. He had seen bulging towels before, and knew that within five minutes of being allotted cubicles, we should have been jumping headlong into icy water.

The sexes were strictly segregated, so that we entered the swimming pool by separate doorways. This puritanical safeguarding of our morals seemed ridiculous to us. We only had to visit one of the Drains or rivers, or walk down to the Seabank, to meet all and sundry transporting themselves in the water, oblivious and uncaring about the anatomical structure of those around them. Large families were also the order of the day, and although so much water surrounded us, the domestic supply often petered out in dry summers, so we relied on a supply brought round the streets by watercart. As this had to be paid for, bathtime in almost every house was a communal affair when we were small. Water was too precious to be wasted, and one bathtub was shared, irrespective of sex.

The majority of us wore hand-me-down costumes which were generally worse for wear, and although they conformed to rule and came down to our knees, they often had holes in places that would not have passed the censor in a chorus line-up. Nevertheless, we ladies had our own doorway at the baths, which led through a conservatory full of tropical plants, including eucalyptus trees, to our pool at the far end. High walls and a lofty roof enclosed it, and as decency and privacy forbade any windows, our only daylight filtered through the grimy glass roofing lights and we swam and frolicked in an eerie twilight Our pool was very small, about half the size of that used by the boys which was in the open air, but both were filled with filtered seawater drawn from the tidal river which flowed past outside.

On my very first visit I was almost frightened out of my wits. I stood dithering on the shallow steps, admiring the antics of those who were floundering in deeper water, when the aged male assistant came up behind me and without the slightest warning, emptied a bucket of water – the residue of wrung-out bathing costumes – over my head. The unexpectedness of the deluge and its weight threw me off balance, and I rolled down the remaining steps and went under. Somebody hauled me upright, coughing and half-blinded by the stinging salt water.

He was a cantankerous old man and that was only one of the tricks he played when he was out of sorts, or peeved by something we had done to annoy him. On one side of the bath, and midway along its length, there was a rope and pulley arrangement to aid would-be swimmers. It was his job to operate this contraption. We put the webbing halter round our bodies, just under the armpits and then backed away from the side to the full extent of the rope. He was supposed to take our weight on the other end, sufficiently to give us buoyancy yet to allow us freedom to work our arms and legs. All went well generally, but there were odd occasions when he would wait until the halter was in position and the optimist in the water was crouched with hands near chest, ready for the first stroke, and then he would give a mighty heave on the rope. The result sent onlookers into fits, for the poor girl would suddenly rise waist high out of the water with her arms still flailing in mid-air, as she literally flew to the side. The episode was not so hilariously funny to the victim, for the sudden jerk put her whole weight onto the wet webbing and it bit into the flesh under the arms, leaving weals that were painful for several days.

The bath was not deep enough for a diving platform or even a springboard, so in lieu of these, a rope was suspended from the roof, and when not in use, was held out of the way in a clip on the far wall. The idea was to grasp the rope with both hands, push off from the side using your feet, and swing out over the heads of the bathers in the water. I never found out what instructional purpose it served, but it was extremely dangerous to those of us who were unlucky enough to be in line with the Tarzan on the end of it. We were either knocked over or received a foot in our faces, unless we kept well to the side and this was not possible when the bath was crowded. It was even worse when the acrobat lost her grip and fell down on top of us.

In time, segregation rules were abolished and we were

allowed to swim with the gentlemen. The ladies' bath was only used for small children and those whose ages and outlines made them bashful.

Chapter 13

GOING TO THE FAIR

The fair came to our town in Maytime, sprawling itself over the Market Place and onto The Green. We looked forward to it for weeks beforehand and one day, my mother would answer the door to a gypsy and her basket of wares. She would thrust forward pegs that she and her family had made, or a colourful bouquet of paper flowers and beg my mother to "Buy them, lady, they'll bring you luck." We knew then that the fair was not far away, for the gypsies were its advance party. They clattered down the street, legs dangling over the sides of their rickety carts and their old-fashioned, high-domed caravans followed behind, overflowing with bright-eyed, tousle-headed children. We ran out to the pavement edge and stared as they passed by. We looked at their outlandish clothes, their gold earrings and swarthy faces. We noticed their high-bridged Roman noses and black ringlets under their old felt hats. They carried with them the foreigner's magic which intrigued us and set us chattering.

We knew that if we behaved ourselves and did not nag, we should be able to cajole Father into taking us to town on Sunday evening, to see the traction engines bringing the fair in. We were never keen to get too close to those hissing,

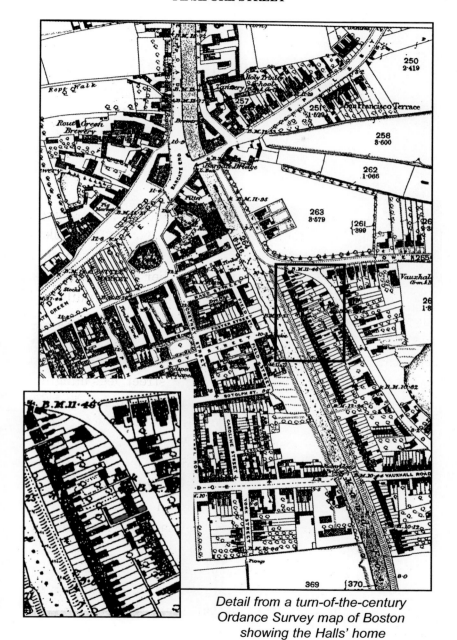

*Detail from a turn-of-the-century
Ordance Survey map of Boston
showing the Halls' home*

L-r: Lavinia, Frances and Kathleen Hall at Skegness (approx) 1928. Frances was born in February 1926.

Annie Hall with her youngest daughter Frances

Annie and Albert Hall pictured in the back garden of their home

Kathleen photographed in a new dress during her stay in Manchester, described in "A Lancashire Lass"

Right:
Annie (left),
Kathleen
(centre) and
Aunt Harriet
of Starling
Cottage
(right).

Below: Top
row l-r, Uncle
Walter, Aunt
Harriet, Sue
Thomas,
Uncle George;
bottom row,
Uncle Fred,
Aunt Ethel,
Uncle Frank
and
Kathleen's
mother Annie
(with the doll).

Skirbeck Tower Road School, Class F, February 1922. Kathleen (aged 7) is in the second row from the front, fourth child from the right, wearing a necklace.

Fishermen on the Maud Foster Drain, c1910. From the local studies collection, Boston Library, by courtesy of Lincolnshire County Council, Education and Cultural Services Department.

Doughty Quay, High Street, Boston, c1914. It was from here that trips 'Down Below' set off. From the local studies collection, Boston Library, by courtesy of Lincolnshire County Council, Education and Cultural Services Department.

The Market Place, Boston. From the local studies collection, Boston Library, by courtesy of Lincolnshire County Council, Education and Cultural Services Department.

clanking monsters while they were jostling their loads into position, but later on, holding on to Father's hands, we liked to thread our way through the stationary chaos and try to identify what had come. Our fair was not just erected and set in motion, it was "Proclaimed". The Mayor in his robes and chain of office, with members of the Corporation and other town dignitaries came out on the balcony of the Town Hall at eleven o'clock precisely the next day. His clerk handed him a scroll from which he read in a suitably loud and impressive manner to the throng of people below, ending "I now proclaim this fair open". Then down he came with his company, leading them through the sightseers to one of the nearby roundabouts, where they enjoyed a free ride.

May fair weather was often lovely. I can remember feeling the warmth of the sun penetrating through my summer dress as we sauntered along enjoying the sights, and how the saddles of the Galloping Horses burned our bare thighs as we sat astride them. If we went on these alone, the 'man' would come and anchor us safely to the brass shaft of our horse with a leather strap. When Father accompanied us, he sat behind and enclosed us with his arms, for the Horses were high off the ground and rotated at speed. We loved to watch the vendor with his tray of jumping beans and usually bought one. The fat lady who stood at the kerbside and manipulated toy rabbits on the end of long lengths of rubber tubing also kept us entranced, but her wares were too pricy for our purses. Our pennies were generally spent on pretty paper balls, suspended on a length of elastic so they could be sent up and down with the palms of our hands like a yo-yo, toffee apples, sticks of rock and tiny celluloid dolls dressed in crepe paper. Sometimes, if Mother thought our stomachs could stand the strain after the evening's mixed bag, we ran into the fish and chip shop on our way home and bought a pennyworth of chips to eat as we went along.

We liked the children's swings, but no-one could persuade us to venture on the big swings, for they were usually sited near a row of tall trees on The Green, and when swung to their fullest extent, almost touched the lower branches.

We watched people on the Cake Walk waltzing and swaying 'no hands' to the music. It looked so easy, so we paid our penny and stepped onto a nightmare! My sister fell flat on her face and had to be rescued by the attendant and lifted over the side to Father. I thought I should be on until the end of the fair. My arms jerked like pistons as I clung to the heaving brass rails. The man kept saying "Move along, please" but my legs wouldn't. It was torture. At last the sheer press of bodies carried me forward and I tumbled out of the gangway in tears.

But we were gluttons for punishment. We took Father, and a coconut that he had won for us, onto the Steam Yachts. These were two huge swinging-boats, netted all round the sides for safety. Both swung their length from a central pivot so that at full swing they literally stood on end. The seats midway were for novices, but we wanted value for money so we sat at the very end, either side of Father who put an arm round us. The boat began to move gently up and gently down. It was lovely to begin with, but the swing became faster and faster, higher and higher, and I let go of my hold on the coconut on an upward flight. It hurtled through the air like a cannon ball and landed with a thwack into the netting at the other end, far below us. When we swung back in reverse, it returned again to us – or to somebody near us. People who were not clinging for dear life to the netting tried to catch it, but without success. By the time we rocked to a standstill, there seemed to be an unanimous opinion about the person who owned the nut, so we nodded in agreement and reeled down the steps without admitting it was ours.

Mother was our companion on the Dragons, the Peacocks and the Gondolas – pronounced 'Gon-dolas' in our part of the world. All three sets were magnificent and favourites with all ages. The ride was smoothly undulating and the last word in comfort. Each carriage held around thirty passengers and encased them in red plush seating and brass scroll work. The scales of the Dragon's and the Peacock's tails were skilful reproductions in brilliant colours and the friezes around the striped canvas tops were masterpieces in paintwork and gold leaf.

Each year, before dismantling, one of these rides, or sometimes the Galloping Horses, would give a Sunday afternoon recital on their steam organ for the benefit of the local hospital. Large crowds gathered to enjoy the music and collecting boxes were liberally filled.

Chapter 14

AWHEEL AND AWAY

Father's livelihood depended upon his bicycle, as did that of everyone who had to travel any distance to his place of employment.

We children learned to balance on roller skates and a small wooden scooter with wobbly wheels, but our initiation into the mysteries of pedal propulsion was both precarious and bloody. Next to swimming, we longed to cycle and as soon as our legs grew long enough and strong enough to rotate the pedals, we never lost a chance of mounting some-body's machine whenever we could. Father's was a constant source of temptation, though the crossbar was a great deterrent to progress. We were told time and again to leave it alone, for the steel pedals gave us bloody shins whenever we slipped off them or the bike heeled over on top of us. Besides these, the oil on the unguarded chain messed up our socks and made bathtime a tearful occasion through the scrubbing that was necessary to clean it off our legs. There were also angry words when Father found the glass broken in his acetylene lamp, through our meddling and letting the bike fall over. However, we persisted in our struggle to ride it and persuaded someone bigger to come with us and steady it, while we crouched crabwise with one leg threaded through and under the crossbar to reach the pedal on the far side. It was a most unbalanced and uncomfortable feat, yet with unflagging practice we managed to 'go alone' for a few yards in triumph.

A lady's bicycle was sometimes ours for the afternoon and we would gather our friends and walk it to Green Lane, well away from parental eyes and any traffic. Turn and turn about we struggled to master the art of steering and getting on and off unaided. One of us, or two if we were small, ran alongside to hold the seat steady. It generally came somewhere near our shoulder blades when we were on the down pedal, and at best only reached the small of our backs on the upward one. There was no sitting properly on the seat, but we wobbled along in seventh heaven all afternoon, oblivious of the heat and dust we were raising. We went home to tea, dusty, sweaty, bruised – and sometimes bleeding and raggy – but happy and boastful of our prowess. Mother never mastered the art, and all because of me. I was four or five years old when she decided to accompany Father one hot summer afternoon to Green Lane to receive instruction on a machine that belonged to a neighbour. She was an apt pupil and made good progress, but I would not sit down in the shade of the hedgerow while she went backwards and forwards along the lane. I insisted on running alongside her like Father, and it was inevitable that I would become tired out, hot and thoroughly 'mardy'. I wept and created to such an extent that in the end my mother suggested, with all the ignorance of a novice, that it wouldn't make a lot of difference if I was hoisted on the carrier behind her. With misgiv-

ings, Father lifted me up and sat me astride, still blubber-
ing. Of course, Mother's weaving progress down the Lane
was made much worse by my weight on the back wheel and
by the fact that I did not keep my legs still. On one run she
outstripped my poor, panting father and after a straight
burst of speed she left the road, made a right-hand curve
over the grassy verge and still pedalling uncontrollably,
descended into a scum-covered dyke, full of foul-smelling
water. She fell off the seat and sank waist deep, while I sat
and shrieked as the water and scum washed over my shoes
and crept up to my knees. Father raced to the rescue and
none too gently, pushed me down on the grass. His sympa-
thies and concern were for my struggling mother. The bike
was none the worse for its ducking, except for its dress-cords
which were festooned with slimy strings of rotting vegeta-
tion. My appearance was not much altered either, but
Mother was a sight to behold – angry, dishevelled, filthy and
dripping from the waist down with dirty water. I had enough
sense to realise I was the cause of the whole fiasco and it
was a very subdued culprit who trotted behind woebegone
parents on the journey home. Mother left us in no doubt that
it was her first and last cycling adventure.

The time came when I began to wish aloud that I had a
bicycle of my own, but it seemed an unlikely prospect in an
era of strikes and short-time working, when sixpence had to
do the work of a shilling. However, word went along the
grapevine that I was saving up and if somebody had a sec-
ond-hand machine to sell, purchase might be considered if
the price was right. I ran errands and was rewarded more
liberally by those in the know, relations were more generous

with parting gifts, and the Rowntree's cocoa tin began to rattle more cheerily with my accumulation of silver threepennies. One day the joyous news was passed over the tea-table that a friend of a friend had a lady's cycle to sell. The selling price of thirty shillings made the offer worth investigation, particularly as my hoard was counted and found to be a little over one pound. I accompanied Mother to view the beauty and I could hardly contain myself during the formalities, before being taken into an enclosed yard by the foolish lady who no longer wanted her treasure. Then we saw it, leaning beside a dolly tub on an outside wall of the wash-house – about seventeen hands high, a vision in black and rust, saggy-seated and with two flat tyres. The remnants of its dirty dress-cords hung down from the rear mudguard and mingled with the spokes of the back wheel. Mother just looked, and I was near to tears, but she was ever an optimist and walked over to give it a closer scrutiny. She thought the price was too much and told the lady so, and after further negotiation it was mine for twenty-five shillings and we walked it back home. Father soon diagnosed its ailments and cured them, and after wooden blocks had been screwed to its pedals so I could reach them, I was awheel and away!

From late spring to early autumn, my father took me with him on fishing trips or, whenever he could spare the time, we cycled through the countryside for miles around. I became familiar with the flat fenland roads which ran before us, unbending and seemingly unending, sometimes for six or seven miles. I can remember the heat of a summer sun that forced us to dismount and seek shade amongst the dusty, waist-high grasses that lined the rutted verges, or beneath

71

a solitary elder or hawthorn, for trees were never plentiful along the roadsides in the Fens.

Sometimes we travelled beside the Drains, re-crossing the same stretch of water as we pedalled the intersecting byways, while Father assessed the fishing possibilities or went to have a word with a fisherman friend he recognised. We kept a lookout for wildlife – hares, rabbits, stoats or weasels – and also for migrating birds, according to the season. The flittermouse, that little acrobat of summer's dusk, sometimes dive-bombed us on the homeward journey.

I learned a lot about crops and often we dismounted and walked a distance along the road to admire or criticise the fields of potatoes or cabbages. We would hang over the gateway of a field of flowering beans and enjoy the honey-sweet smell, and Father sometimes drew my attention to a saffron patch shining afar in the sunlight, which I knew was flowering mustard. He would lie full stretch on the grass verge and enjoy a cigarette while I foraged in the wheat by a field gate, looking for poppies and blue scabious that grew there.

We waited at crossing gates for the passing of goods trains and I counted the wagons and waved to the guard. Sometimes Father stopped to chat to a crossing keeper he knew, for his work often took him to the lonely gatehouses. There were times when we exchanged weather prophesies with a tramp, sitting beside his bundles on a heap of chippings by the roadside. A great event was to come upon a gypsy camp in a shady lane, though the rush of suspicious dogs unnerved me and we had to ride carefully to avoid wandering broods of bantams.

The roads were usually solitary and we were able to pedal

side by side, talking and looking around us, without much fear of traffic. We shared the highways for the most part with other cyclists, usually farmhands riding bent-backed with their insteps on the pedals and knees turned out, swaying with each downward thrust and making heavy weather of the journey, or with carrier's carts, pony traps and farm wagons. Occasionally we dismounted and gave way to a motorcar belonging to some enterprising farmer, and coughed in the dust cloud that enveloped us after it passed.

On one occasion we accompanied the Maud Foster Drain for several straight miles to Cowbit and then on again, until we came to a small cluster of dwellings known as Mount Pleasant. We crossed the stone bridge to enter a small churchyard and just a few paces to the left of the gateway my father pointed to a gravestone. It marked the burial place of his father who died when my own father was a boy. Grandfather had been a farmer and I thought, as I stood there, how fitting it was that one who had loved the quiet countryside, should lie within a yard or two of a wheat field. Sun shone down through the trees onto the old green stone, and I wondered what my father's thoughts were as we stood together, reading the inscription.

We travelled the Droves, Pullovers and Rampers – old Fen names for desolate, back of beyond places, where the bitter wind on a winter's day could make your face numb. Occasionally we left the roads altogether and rode precariously along the top of the Seabank until we reached Down Below and I stood there, literally leaning against the wind as it blew in from the Deeps. It was weird and lonely, and not a place to fish alone, especially in wintertime. The blue, oozy mud was treacherous and sucked at Father's waders almost like quicksand. All kinds of flotsam rode on the swell, some of it macabre like the upturned carcase of a sheep, stiff-legged and sodden, which rose and fell, twisted and turned and was then released on the crest of yet another wave to ride onward towards the open sea. Father caught dabs and occasionally a conger eel, as sinuous as the grass snake and with a body as thick as a man's wrist. It writhed and lunged so that the line shrieked from the reel and became hopelessly tangled around its victim.

Wild geese with necks outstretched flew in V-formation above our heads, while gulls rose and planed or stood by the water's edge in conclave with strange waders which we could not identify – birds from overseas, resting on their journeying.

Chapter 15

MY DRINK IS WATER BRIGHT

My friend Mabel was a tall, freckle-faced tomboy, several years older than the majority of us who played with her in the passageway and around the houses. She was a foster child and lived with an elderly lady who was deeply religious and fanatically opposed to any liquid refreshment stronger than tea. She was rather forbidding, slightly stooping with the years and always dressed in black clothes that had seen better days on other people.

Where she found the children's clothes I do not know. We all felt sorry for Mabel who was often dressed in heavy serge frocks, far too long or far too short, but never just right. In summer she wore monstrosities that even a pinafore could not hide, all frills and flounces which looked so droll on a girl who could shin up a tree like a boy. Mabel's brother capered in the summer sunshine wearing sailor suits and buttoned boots and was the laughing stock of other lads at school, who sometimes made him weep. Mabel did her best to make adjustments to some of these outlandish garments and was perpetually in trouble with her foster mother who saw in her a rebellious spirit and signs of 'worldliness', which led to warnings that such vanity would be her undoing. Mabel was hard to convince and the thought of being the devil's hand-maiden later on did not seem to trouble her in the least.

She was a daredevil and was usually one of the party when we congregated in Green Lane to play 'Mothers and Fathers' in the bottom of a dry dyke which was sheltered completely from prying eyes by an overhang of briars. Her size and bossiness generally won her the role of Mother. Besides, she was the one who had sufficient nerve to push a way through the gappy hedge that ran alongside the dyke and gather a few handfuls of gooseberries and soft fruit from a nurseryman's bushes. This provender, together with several bottles of water, made housekeeping more realistic, though the delayed effects of the berries were sometimes far from pleasant, and puzzled our mother.

Through my friendship with Mabel, I went on the stage. Her foster mother, besides being a campaigner for teetotalism, was an ardent chapel-goer and her contribution to its social life took the form of training young members to sing and take part in 'suitable' sketches, usually about rescuing drunkards or maidens from the path of unrighteousness. We met round her deal-topped table under the plopping gas mantle – boys, girls and infants, the shy, the show-offs and those who tried in more senses than one. We practised and sulked and struggled, and after weeks of endeavour, mumps, measles or some other scourge would scythe through the cast and lay us low. There would be panic action to recast the leads, and trouble off-stage on the night if any of the convalescent players turned up, whey-faced, and thwarted their understudies, particularly if the proud mothers of both parties were sitting out front. We faced the audience with hands behind our backs, stomachs well out and swayed to the beat of the opening verse.

My drink is water bright,
Water bright, water bright,
My drink is water bright
From the Celestial spring!

As the chapel stood in Pump Square, I always thought it a most appropriate song. Sometimes I deserted Mabel and her foster mother and went with two other friends and their mother to a different 'water party'. Everyone who belonged wore a white enamelled brooch in the form of a ribbon bow, but I never found what this signified, or indeed, what religious denomination they all supported. We sang hymns, said prayers and listened to denunciations of the demon drink by visiting speakers. I learned all about gin palaces and the evil spirits which lived in bottles, and came home relieved to find my mother enjoying a cup of Mazawattee tea.

Mother put us on the water wagon almost as soon as we were born, by signing the Pledge on our behalf with the Sons of Temperance. As soon as I was old enough to attend the weekly meetings of the junior section, the superintendent and his wife welcomed me into the fold. We had much to thank them for, as they laboured hard and enthusiastically to make the fellowship a happy and instructive one. We conducted our own meetings with their guidance, and elected our officers in the same way as the adult section of the movement. In time, I learned to wield the gavel and keep the minute book. We wore replicas of the adult regalia, collarettes of red velvet, edged with gold braid and bearing the round badge of the Order, worked in gold thread with a swinging gold tassel.

The annual event we all looked forward to was the Chrysanthemum Show. As soon as the subject came up for discussion at one of our meetings, or when the letter arrived from the nurseryman that the cuttings he was donating were ready for despatch, we began to plan our horticultural programme.

My sister and I made a surreptitious sortie behind Father's shed among his useful junk of buckets, bowls and oil drums. We were uninterested in the bowls and recoiled from the drums because these were used for mixing liquid manure for tomato plants or as hatching nurseries for his gentles. Our aim was to lay claim to four strong-sided, leaky buckets from among those with too-rusty rims and crumbling bottoms, which we knew would collapse if we loaded them with dirt. It was always something of a dare to grab the buckets and get the cuttings safely planted before Father found out, for they were his potato buckets which he used on the allotment. We knew it and he knew we knew it! There was generally a bit of stamping around when he found we had made a surprise attack on his preserves, but though he threatened to "up-ship the whole lot!", we knew that he did not really mean it, and of course, he never did such a thing.

On one or two occasions, when our tongues slipped and we let Mother know about our impending planting session, we found our plans had been leaked and the coveted potato buckets were missing. Then the laugh was on us, but nobody said anything. It would have been certain disaster to put our precious cutttings into the garden, for its boundaries were open to the wide world and it was a regular convenience for cats and dogs in the neighbourhood.

We even had disastrous seasons with the buckets. A yard brush would be propped close by, slip and decapitate one of our budding prizewinners, or somebody would forget they were lined up close by the house wall, charge outside into the darkness and get a reminder on their shins. We would then hear the offending bucket getting anything but preferential treatment.

Sometimes a lusty specimen would droop into decline before our eyes, though we struggled for its life as long as there was anything showing above the soil. Father was consulted in a difficult diagnosis, but more often than not, the result was one potato bucket to him. One thing he would not do was to take any hand himself in rearing the plants. He considered it unfair, as the Show prizes were awarded for care given by the children themselves, and he was careful to explain that the whole idea was to encourage us to rear something beautiful and have the joy of knowing we had done all the work. Whether we won a prize or not didn't matter, he said. We believed him, but there was always a vast difference between the flowers in the prize-winning buckets and the ones in ours. Some entries in the Best Disbudded Blooms section bore heads equal in size and curliness to the exquisite specimens displayed in florists' windows, and we were amazed at the cleverness of our victorious Brothers and Sisters.

A few days before the Show we paid a visit to Marks & Spencer's Penny Bazaar in the Market Place and chose what we thought would be the most eye-catching crepe paper roll.

With Mother's help, we cut it to size and made flutes along the edges by alternately stretching and nipping with our fingers, and then wrapped each bucket carefully. The finishing touch was a fancy drape, made by folding the paper lengthwise to form a sash, and this was swathed around the middle of the buckets and tied into a bow at the focal point of its positioning on the stage.

Then Father came to the rescue. On the night before the Show, he loaded our buckets into a pram and with us on either side, helping to push, propelled it to the Church Hall. We passed the lamp-lighter on his round, with his long rod over his shoulder, its little light flickering at the top as he strode away in front of us. At street corners we began to meet other groups of children with their press-ganged parents, trundling pramloads of blooms, and bigger boys and girls with wheelbarrows full of flowers, all heading the same way. We tried to assess the merits of their loads under the little circles of gaslight and, of course, they were just as curious about our pramful.

The following night we all knew. We passed through the glass doors and were momentarily dazzled by the brightness of tier upon tier of chrysanthemums which faced us along the whole width of the stage, down to floor level. As soon as we could get near enough to the exhibits, we read the details on the prize cards propped in front of the winning entries and identified their owners. We searched along the rows for our also-rans, but in spite of the distinctive crepe paper, we sometimes searched in vain. Father had been right, as it didn't seem to matter very much, and we were going to enjoy ourselves.

After the presentations and votes of thanks, we sat back for the concert which had been arranged by the superintendent and his wife. There was music and often a magic act, but for some reason, I remember the lady elocutionist best. She came on the stage and in faultless diction, with superb expression of voice, face and hands, delivered streams of story-verse that left us mesmerised. It was like listening to half a dozen different people conversing together through one mouth. She was the highlight of the evening's entertainment for me, as I thought of my own struggles to memorise my lines in Pump Square.

After the concert ended, many willing hands pushed the wooden seats aside, leaving plenty of clear space for organised games. Everyone who was old enough joined in the fun, while grown-ups chatted and enjoyed the tea and cakes which were brought round.

The only thing I cannot remember clearly, perhaps because of a guilty conscience, is who was the pram-pusher with the buckets of rejects on the way home. I expect it was poor Mother!

Chapter 16

GIRL GUIDES

As well as being our meeting place on cookery days and for Sunday School, the church hall was our venue on many social occasions. One of these was the weekly gathering of Girl Guides and Brownies. My knowledge of these two movements came just too late for me to be a Brownie, so I begged my mother to let me be a Guide.

The biggest deterrent was the price of the uniform. This consisted of a navy felt hat with an enormous brim, a tunic-type blouse worn over a pleated skirt, and of course, the requisite badges, shoulder flashes, leather belt with appendages, lanyard, necktie and a pair of white cotton gloves to be worn on ceremonial occasions. I acquired my uniform bit by bit, through secondhand bargains from those who left, until I became the proud possessor of the whole. I was not at all conspicuous during the transition stages, as most of my colleagues were in a similar predicament, and it was a motley company who marched in church parades behind the town band. Those who were resplendent in full-dress uniform were usually placed in the outside lanes to detract attention from the more penurious members in the middle.

One of the highlights during my time with the Guides was when Her Royal Highness the Princess Royal inspected contingents from all parts of Lincolnshire, in the beautiful grounds of a mansion on the outskirts of Lincoln.

For weeks beforehand we were lectured on behaviour and etiquette in case the Great Lady spoke to us, and we in turn, badgered our mothers to save up faster for the still missing pieces of uniform that we needed. My worry was the lack of a pair of black shoes, and though Mother commiserated with me, a new pair was quite out of the question. The night before the great event, Father came to the rescue with a bottle of black dye and transformed my one and only brown pair.

The following morning, of course, it rained. When our bus squelched and slithered its way through a field gate to join the fleet of buses already there, it was pouring in torrents. The wide hat brims did little more than keep our ears dry, and by the time we found our place on the inspection ground, we were bedraggled and rat-tailed, for our hair was either worn long and loose or in pigtails. It was little consolation that when Royalty was due to inspect our ranks, a watery sun came out from behind the clouds in her honour. The grass began to steam and so did we. I looked at my feet to make sure they were in line with the rest and nearly passed out with shame. My newly-blacked shoes had gone piebald. The reaction of the dye in contact with the sodden grass had turned the toecaps a dirty white, while black and brown splodges covered the rest of the uppers. I didn't know what to do. I told the girl next to me and she began to giggle and passed the news along the line so that heads craned forward to inspect the phenomenon. I tried to arrange my feet so that they were partially hidden in the tufty grass, but I need not have worried. The Princess was in such animated conversation with the Lady Commissioner when she passed by, that she didn't even know I was there. I felt sick with relief and said a silent prayer of thankfulness.

Later in the day, as rain clouds gave way to really warm sunshine, we were moved to a grassy terrace and told to fold our mackintoshes under us, and busy ourselves with the needlework specimens we had brought along. Other contingents were similarly employed with raffia, canework or bobbin lace. Her Royal Highness was expected to come amongst us and inspect any handiwork that took her fancy.

I covered my colourful shoes with my skirt and drew my knapsack from my back to get out the linen table mat with its half-finished motif of lazy daisies. Instructions were that if the Princess came by, we were to spread our work in front of our knees so she could see it at a glance. She eventually came out of the mansion behind us and threaded her way among various groups, then I saw she was heading in the direction of my little circle. We spread our work on the grass and sat still, excited and hopeful. She stooped to pick up the work of a Guide on the far side, but as she straightened up again, she stepped back a pace or two and unknowingly, heeled my lazy daisies into the wet turf before moving away. It was not my day. Enough was enough and I was not at all sorry when the time came to scramble back into the bus and go home.

Camping was often talked about and read about. The local Scouts went off once a year with their tents but we had to be satisfied with 'camp fire' singsongs in the church hall. A mock fire was concocted from sticks and red paper and we sat around it on the wooden floor and let our imaginations do the rest.

To our surprise and delight, there came a day when we were told we were going to camp, not under canvas, but at a farm some five miles out of town. Blankets and a pillow were all that was needed. Palliasses – new potato sacks stuffed with chaff – would be waiting at the other end. A local builder offered to loan two of his handcarts and we were to pile our possessions onto them, then taking it in turns, groups of us were to push these to the camping site.

That summer we awoke day after day to cloudless skies and broiling heat. It was the end of July and when Father heard of the transport arrangements he was livid at "such foolishness". He was in the building trade himself and had helped to push many a heavily-laden handcart. The thought of a bunch of children struggling with two of them in the summer heat along five miles of dusty roads, made his blood boil, particularly as the village had its own railway station and could be reached by train several times a day at the cost of a few pence. As far as he was concerned, I was to go by train or stop at home. I wept but he was immovable, so I canvassed around for a partner brave enough to go the easy way. Everyone I asked felt as I did, that to funk the rigours of the road would probably mean excommunication or being sent to Coventry in the camp, but I had reckoned without Mabel. She thought it was a grand joke and laughed herself silly.

Father slung our rolls of bedding over his crossbar and

saw us safely into the Guard's van. It was only a few minutes' journey. We knew the village and found that the farm was not far from the station.

An old man was bending down filling buckets at a pump in the centre of the farmyard as we shyly edged in, clutching our bundles to our stomachs. He straightened up and with "'ello, young 'uns. Didn't expect yer just yet," beckoned us into a stable on the far side. We sidled after him and dropped our rolls on to the pile of fat potato sacks he indicated. "Go where yer like, but keep away from the 'oss pond", said our guide, leaving us with a wave of his hand, and we did.

We toured the village, had a peep inside the church and bought ourselves some aniseed balls to suck as we sat in the shade of a hawthorn to watch the road, as yet empty, for signs of our comrades.

We saw them first as a little dust-storm in the far distance; a 'disturbance' that did not seem to move any nearer for a long, long time. Mabel was in high spirits and was all for prancing down the road to meet them. She took some restraining, but we waited beneath the tree. It was just as well. The bigger girls round the first handcart were shouldering their bundles, and two prostrate little forms lay on top of the remainder that were piled in it. Shoes and stockings up to the knees were powdered white with dust. The heavy felt hats hung down between shoulder blades by their elastic chin straps. Some girls, in ill-fitting shoes, limped along with blistered heels, and all were dirty and tired out.

Expressions of astonishment and querulous criticism met us from those who had enough breath and energy to bother. I timidly approached the Leader, "Please, Miss, my father made us come by train". She glowered at me and shepherded the toiling company slowly round the last bend and into the farmyard. Mabel and I fell in at the rear, with relief on my part that at least the first encounter was over.

Reflection must have shown our Leader the sense of Father's decision. The handcarts eventually found their way home up-ended in the farmer's pig float, and when the time came, we all travelled back with our bundles on the train.

Chapter 17

SUMMER IN THE SUNSHINE

Summer holidays in fenland schools were always longer than those for schools in industrial areas, as children were needed on the farms to help gather in the late potato harvest.

My country friends looked forward to these labouring days in the fresh air and never seemed to find the hours long or the work arduous. Although their hands were small, they could stoop more easily and move more quickly than the grown-ups, and the shillings they earned were put to good use in providing them with stout boots and warm, serviceable clothing, so necessary for trudging or cycling along cold fen roads in winter.

They congregated with their elders in the flat, wind-swept fields, wearing their oldest clothes and a sacking apron if the ground was claggy and the buckets muddy. They moved to their allotted stretches, usually working in pairs, and along these the flailing arms of the spinner rotated, cleaving into the black soil and throwing the potatoes clear for them to gather up. There was no time for dalliance, as the spinner was a quick worker and any potatoes still ungathered were likely to be re-buried when it came round again to unearth another row. Buckets were filled and then emptied into tall two-handled mollys standing at strategic points in the field. These were unloaded into farm carts and the potatoes taken away for examination and grading, before being stored in long clamps adjacent to the field gates.

We, too, left the dusty roads, our marbles, skipping ropes and whips and tops, for the fields and shady hedgerows of Green Lane. There we chased and climbed to our hearts' content, making friends with the horses by beguiling them to the gate with a handful of pulled grasses, and festooning their foreheads with branches of elder to drive away the flies that pestered their eyes. We played in the dry dyke bottoms and threw ourselves down in the shade with a favourite book or new comic when we were tired. The hot sun and wind, with the scent of the sea on its breath, soon burnished our limbs, bleached our hair and sent us home each day content and ravenously hungry. My special country friend who came home with me every day in wintertime to eat a hot dinner, instead of having sandwiches in a cold cloakroom, invited me to stay with her during the summer holiday. She had no brothers or sisters and no father. He had been killed in the Great War, only a week or two before she was born, but she treasured his photographs and had an unusual keepsake. It was a man's white linen milking apron, neatly rolled and tied, just as he had left it after wearing it for the last time. It made me sad to see her standing with it in her hands, caressing it with her fingers.

Her mother had been left to carry on the small farmstead with the help of an aged relative and casual labour. It was chiefly arable but dairy cattle grazed the banks of the Drain and pigs and chickens inhabited the orchard. Oh, the happy memories of that orchard!

There was an old dilapidated coach resting on its shafts under one of the ancient apple trees. Its windows were intact but the doors swung back on broken strap hinges and the mouldy stuffing in its seats made cosy roosting places for the hens. We always felt carefully inside the holes in the upholstery for their eggs before starting our games, for more than once we nearly sat down on a newly-laid breakfast. Two beautiful brass carriage lamps, still intact with the remains of tallow candles in their sockets, adorned the front, beside the box seat. We lit the candles, climbed up onto the high box and with labouring whip, spurred phantom horses on desperate journeys. Many a bullet ricocheted on the doors as we tied them with string and crouched behind them when crossing imaginary prairies. More than one highwayman held us up with a water pistol. It was a constant source of pleasure in our do-or-dare games, and took us in elegant state to many a mythical ball, dressed up in trailing frocks and stilt-heeled shoes. As the farmstead stood by the roadside, en route to a favourite weekend picnic spot, and was also adjacent to a Drain which was lined with fishermen on Sundays, my friend's mother opened her small parlour as a shop and stocked it with sweets, soft drinks, cigarettes and tobacco. In the height of summer she served ice-cream in little glasses, and cups of tea at tables under the orchard trees. Customers were glad to relax in the shade and enjoy these refreshments, and the fishermen soon reduced the stocks of cigarettes and pipe tobacco. It was fun for us to act as waitresses and trot in and out of the house with trays. The sight of a silver threepenny or even a penny hiding beneath a saucer when we cleared away the empties, was ample reward for the piles of washing-up that followed.

We played hide and seek round the thickets that grew along the top of the banks and helped the old man to round up the cattle at milking time. We gathered eggs from all sorts of unlikely places in the orchard and washed and counted them into dozens, ready for sale in the town dairies.

The old man filled and ticketed the milk churns each morning, and loaded them into a pony trap to take them into town. In the summertime he started his journey when the sun still struggled to pierce the heat haze in the orchard trees. We rose early too and helped him to catch the pony and harness it, and made sure that his whip was in its stock. When it was the day of my departure, I climbed in beside him, taking presents of eggs and cream cheeses, wrapped in cabbage leaves, for my mother. He fastened the door of the trap, flicked the reins lightly along the pony's back and away we went through the gateway, over the stone bridge and down the narrow country road, startling sparrows and pinging flints from under the spinning wheels into the hedgerows. Farmhands called out "Nice morning" as we passed them on their bicycles, going to their day's labour in the fields. Bedroom curtains were still drawn across the windows of most of the houses when we reached the outskirts of town, and the streets were empty and peaceful.

Mother was up and Father had already gone to work. She had heard the 'clop-clop' of the pony's hooves and was at the door to greet us. The old man passed my bundles and presents to Mother across the garden fence. She tried to entice him indoors for a pot of tea, but he was anxious to reach the dairy on time and the pony was restless, jangling her bit, so we waved goodbye and watched him out of sight, before going into the house to exchange our news.

Chapter 18

THE SEABANK

Sometimes on a lovely, warm afternoon, Mother would forget about housework and take us down to the Seabank. We foraged in the shoe cupboard for our oldest sandshoes to paddle in, then ran to the towel drawer and rolled up the pieces of towelling that were kept ready for these excursions. Mother cut sandwiches and flasks were filled. Father's tea was laid ready for when he came home and a note was written to tell him where we had gone.

There were alternate routes – one round by the road and the other alongside the Drain. We usually chose the latter because it was more direct and we also knew Mother would be less likely to meet a gossip and delay us.

As soon as we saw the Seabank ahead, we left her behind and scrambled up its steep side to the top, and then filled our eyes with the beauty all around us. A blue expanse of sky above our heads, the wide, green carpet of marshes spread at our feet, crisscrossed with creeks which we knew to our cost were alive with soldier crabs at low tide. Beyond, the broad river, winking and rippling its way from the Deeps to fill the dock basin which lay hidden from us behind a curve in the bank. We shaded our eyes to catch a glimpse of the tops of the tall cranes and listened to engines shunting and clanging the railway trucks in the sidings on the wharves.

We turned about and tracked the bank, the saltings and the river until they vanished together into the shimmering heat haze, far away on the horizon. Only the tower of a lovely old church thrust above the bank a few hundred yards from us, and stood like a benediction against the skyline. Its ancient churchyard lay low on the other side. A sister of one of my school friends was buried there and I remember peering into the grave before her interment and seeing a floating carpet of grass clippings that had been thrown into it to hide the salt water seepage from the eyes of the mourners.

Small bushes grew here and there along the seaward side of the bank, and Mother found shade by one of these and began to unpack the baskets. We stripped to vest and knickers and squelched our way through the sea pinks to the shallow water in the creeks. More often than not we came face to face there with some of our school friends and the day was made for all of us.

It was possible to reach the water's edge along a broad track of hard-baked sand when the tide was right out, but once it began to turn again it was too risky to stay. Water oozed up through the soft, blue mud which anchored the green growth and trickled insidiously into the creeks. Before we realised it, the safe way back could vanish, even though we were standing on a platform of hard sand which was still dry behind it. Mother accompanied us once, pushing my sister in the pram, and we became stranded and had to be rescued by some men with a rowing boat, who ferried us to safety, pram and all. Some of the wider creeks were spanned by single plank bridges which became slippery to cross when awash, or when wet with the traffic of paddling feet. Though wide, none of the creeks was very deep, and when filled to the brim, they were deceptive. Local bathers were aware of the danger of diving into them, but strangers sometimes saw the water lapping the planks, misjudged its depth and came to grief. Occasionally on a sunny Sunday afternoon, we climbed aboard a horse-drawn wagonette in the Market Place and enjoyed a jog-trot journey along five miles of quiet country roads, to rendezvous with the same Seabank further along the coastline. We clip-clopped past my friend's farmstead and wound our way through the main street of a village which lay half a mile beyond, and which marked the half-way stage of our journey. No-one bothered to 'chirrup' the horse and he picked his own pace along the rutty roads. We sat warm and drowsy on the bench seats behind him, too lazy even to chatter. The sun-soaked fields slipped slowly by until at last we arrived at the journey's end. Bicycles, pony traps, other wagonettes and the occasional motor car were already parked on the roadside verges near the bank. The hokey-pokey men and fruit vendors were doing a roaring trade from their pitches in the shade of the Hotel wall. The sound of laughter and clapping came down on the wind from the Hotel gardens where a concert party was giving its usual weekend performance.

We did not paddle on Sundays, but walked with Father over the sun-baked mud to examine the old wooden hulk which lay on its side near the waterline, barnacled, bleached and breaking up bit by bit with every tide that washed over it. We left it to Mother to walk in a leisurely way down to a row of coastguards' cottages, low in the lea of the bank, and stake a claim to one of the trestle tables which were set up in each of the small front gardens. Pots of tea were in great demand and earned the ladies in the houses an addition to their housekeeping throughout the summer. Patrons were welcome to eat their own food at the tables and order pots of tea to be brought out to them. Mother's order was taken and the tea awaited us on our return, together with all the good things in the picnic basket.

Mother loved a picnic and as far as she was concerned, nothing was too much trouble to make it a success, but Father did not favour eating alfresco meals "covered in flies", or where every mouthful became a risk because of wasps. Neither did he relish an audience of strangers. An incident occurred on the sands during a day at the seaside that put him off picnics for ever. As usual, Mother packed far too much food and remembering his preference for eating in a civilised manner, a tablecloth, cutlery and crockery as well. He was "fit to drop" after carrying all this around until it was needed, and even accepted the site she chose, adjacent to the promenade which was thronged with strollers. We sat around the spread, waiting for her to pour tea from the flasks, when we felt the first heavy spots from a black cloud above us, which had been lolling over the beach for most of the afternoon. Mother "didn't think it would be much", but almost as she said it, down came a deluge. The promenaders ran for the shelters and the crowds on the beach stampeded in all directions. Mother shrieked to my sister and me to grab two piled-up plates each and run. We struggled across the sand, up the ramp and along the promenade, leaving a picnic trail behind us. The shelterers were in fits over our capers, and one in the front row rolled his newspaper to flag us in and began to shout the odds on the three runners. Father was livid when he came in a poor third and lined up alongside us with his plates.

We thought we were luckier than our poor mother who was still on the sands, throwing crockery into the picnic baskets. As I said to Father, there was only her and the donkeys left on the beach, but he muttered, looking the wag in the eye, "One blithering ass got away!" A kind lady relieved him of his plates and lent him her umbrella so that he could fetch Mother. She staggered in with the chaotic jumble in the baskets, wet through and thoroughly wilted.

The rainstorm ceased as suddenly as it had begun and the crowd surged out of the shelter and left it to us. We sank down on the slatted seat and picked at the soggy remnants of the feast. Mother poured tea into the cups and we sipped in silence. Nobody looked at Father and nobody enjoyed the rest of that day. Only a long time afterwards could we see its funny side. Father never saw it.

Chapter 19

DIGGING AND DELVING

Father's love of the land found an outlet in his allotment, and next to fishing, gardening was his favourite pastime. He loved the smell of newly-turned soil and always said it acted like a tonic when he felt jaded in mind or body.

His patch of land was originally the bed of a large pond and the outline of its diameter was clearly seen in the dished contour of the ground. The soil was therefore moist and loamy and yielded all sorts of small surprises through the years. We collected a number of ancient coins, one of which was a replica of a golden guinea, but was in fact a medallion bearing the words "In memory of the Good Old Days" on its reverse side. Sheep's jawbones, bleached and bare, came grinning to the surface on the spade, to frighten us and make us jump back in alarm. On one occasion, Father unearthed a small flintlock pistol, beautifully engraved and intact except for the hammer which had eroded and broken off during its long burial. We wondered if it had been the weapon in some dastardly deed of long ago.

By far the most delightful surprise, and one that kept us enthralled for a long time afterwards, was that which Father brought home to us one Saturday teatime, in a small basket.

He had dislodged it while uprooting an elder tree which had grown of its own accord near the raspberry canes and was preventing light from reaching them. When we peeped inside the basket we saw a soft, greyish-white ball of fur, as large as a football. Father lifted it gently on to the path and parted it so we could see inside. There lay five helpless creatures, curled up together and so tiny that we could hardly believe him when he told us they were baby rabbits. Mother found a shoebox and using the natural nest to line it, transferred them in and put in inside the fender for warmth. We helped her feed them all through the days that followed, with lukewarm milk from a fountain pen filler, pushing the rubber tip into their mouths and squeezing droplets down their throats. To everyone's surprise, they thrived on the treatment and it was not long before they were strong enough to be put into a wooden hutch in a sheltered corner of the yard. From then on they were our concern and they kept us busy, searching down Green Lane for plantain and dandelion roots to augment the cornmeal and oats that Mother made into a mash for them.

We loved rabbit pie, but they had nothing to fear, and just in case the grown-ups had ideas in that direction, we counted our darlings each night and again in the mornings.

We loved to go with Father to the allotment during warm summer evenings and on Saturday afternoons to play in the sunshine while Mother went off to town to do shopping. She often joined us in the early evening and gave a hand with the weeding or planting out. We stayed on until well after sunset, when the dew began to fall and made us shiver, and we could see a ground mist, as white as milk, creeping over the fields beyond Love Lane.

Access to the allotments was through a field gate and then along a wide ribbon of turf which separated the gardens from a dyke. In summertime, this was quite dry and completely hidden by overhanging elder trees and hawthorn bushes. This green tunnel was shady and secretive, and we took our dolls and miniature tea-sets and played houses, raiding Father's peas, carrots or soft fruit, according to the season. On the other side of the hedgerow were the kitchen gardens of large houses which lined the residential road where we attended Sunday School, and level with Father's allotment was one full of fruit and nut trees. A large Victoria plum tree spread its arms right over the hedge and dangled its luscious fruit just above our heads. As it was impossible for the owner to straddle the hedge to gather them, he gave us permission to pick them, and we enjoyed its bounty in many a pot of home-made jam in wintertime. He was equally generous with the filberts which fell into the dyke bottom, and these were collected and carefully stored for Christmas festivities.

Father loved animals, especially dogs, and we had a succession of them through my childhood, but he expected obedience from them as he did from us; they knew this and responded when he spoke to them. All except Bob. He was an all-white, longhaired mongrel with a tail that curled over his rump like a fluffy pompom – an amiable fool who was easily led and quite incapable of learning anything. He drove Father to distraction with his stupidity. He could not be trusted anywhere and was usually in disgrace, so whenever he came with us to the allotment, he had to be tethered for his own good.

About three hundred yards away from Father's plot was Love Lane, a winding country track which separated the allotment ground from arable and pasture land. In one of the latter fields, sheep were grazing one Saturday afternoon when we took Bob with us. Father tethered him as usual and he and I went to the far end of the garden to gather raspberries. We had hardly started to pick the canes when bedlam broke loose in the lane and, of course, Bob joined in. We straightened up and were astonished to see a pack of dogs enter the field in full cry and begin to chase and savage the sheep. Father dropped the fruit chip and dragging me after him, made for Bob who was going berserk and, no doubt, barking instructions for the other dogs to wait for him. We had a terrible tussle for he was a big dog and very determined to join in the fun. In the end, Father had to rope his legs together and carry him bodily the length of the allotments and then walk him all the way home. That was the last time he ever came with us.

There was almost a club atmosphere among the allotment men. Tools were borrowed and lent freely; seeds, advice and help were given by one and all and no excess produce ever went to waste if there were others who could make good use of it. The children on the other plots were our playfellows and many of them attended the same school. Commiseration, a little boasting and a competitive spirit gave punch to the hard work. It was good to stand, before leaving for home, and admire our King Edward potatoes all in flower and level as a tabletop, especially if they were taller and greener than those growing on either side.

No plot was left untended during the illness of a gardener. It became the joint responsibility of the rest and was planted and weeded so that when he came back in due course, it was tidy and in good heart. In the case of long and serious illnesses when foods needed by the absent friend strained his family budget, there would be a collection and the money would be pushed anonymously through his letterbox.

Father allocated to us a small strip of garden near the grass verge and tossed seed packet remainders our way, in the hope that we would become interested in sowing and growing. We always started full of enthusiasm and goodwill, but neither lasted very long. My bossy sister purloined the tools that I wanted, and her bossy sister took the lion's share from the seed packets. If we got beyond that stage, once the sun began to shine, weeding became a bore and our seedlings were left to struggle for survival in a thicket of chickweed, while we played merrily in the dyke. Father eventually realised the futility of trying to interest us in serious agricultural endeavour, re-dug the strip and gave it to his cabbage plants.

Chapter 20

STARLING COTTAGE

Mother was born a Lincolnshire 'yellow belly' and except for a short migration into Lancashire with Father, during which time I was born, she spent all her married life in her birthplace of Boston, in close proximity to several of her married brothers and sisters. One of these was Aunt Harriet who lived in Starling Cottage and, upon our return from the north, she offered us a temporary home until we found Number Ten.

I loved her and her house. She was small and plump with a mass of strong, black hair which she combed back from her forehead and wore in a coiled bun on the crown of her head. Starling Cottage was a long, three-storey building, standing far back from the road and facing its own orchard and garden. Her brother and his family lived in the adjoining building, and it was said the two houses had originally been one large residence. This probably accounted for the fact that the main windows and frontage of both houses faced the opposite way from the other houses nearby, which were built later in the grounds of the old Hall. The weathering of the red brickwork, the ornate chimney stacks and the quaintness of structural features inside both cottages, certainly indicated their antiquity.

As soon as I was old enough to make the journey alone from Number Ten, I was a constant visitor on summer evenings and at weekends. I sometimes arrived on Sunday mornings before she and Uncle Dick had had their breakfast

I opened the wall gate and ran along the narrow path beneath a huge pear tree and between herbaceous borders, and burst into the kitchen to find Uncle on his knees with a box of sticks and a scuttle of coal, lighting the fire in the range. Aunt was busy at the gas stove, preparing their breakfast. Sunday was a go-as-you-please day with them and I settled myself in the fireside chair and told them my news as they sat down to enjoy their eggs and bacon.

If the fire was already alight and rosy when I arrived, one of them would hand me a round of bread, the toasting fork and butter dish, and I squatted on the snip rug and enjoyed a second breakfast. We switched on the two-valve battery set which stood on a table by the window and listened to the reedy voices from 2LO, or to singing being relayed from a Morning Service. If it was wintertime, I sat on my chair, snug by the fireside and talked to Aunt as she did her kitchen chores and prepared dinner. She knew I had come to spend the day with them, and more often than not, when tea-time came round, she would climb on to a little footstool and reach up to the high shelf in her store cupboard to bring down a tin of sardines, for she knew they were my great favourites.

The orchard and garden were lovely from early spring-time until late autumn. Aconites, snowdrops, crocus, white and purple violets and masses of daffodils took turns in ringing the feet of the fruit trees, and they too scented the air with their clouds of pink blossom. Black Diamond and Victoria plum trees rubbed branches with those of the Codlings and Russets, and together they sheltered the long lines of Lloyd George raspberry canes and currant and gooseberry bushes planted beneath them. A towering pear tree stood near the gate and tantalised Uncle every autumn with its crown of golden pears that dangled out of reach of the longest ladder. They had to be left to fall eventually, and exploded with a loud and juicy thwack on the path below, or as sometimes happened, on the luckless head of a passer-by.

The old brick pig sties in the far corner of the garden provided a snug retreat for White Leghorns and Rhode Island Red hens which strutted and cackled in their wire runs and provided Aunt with eggs for her deep custards and pots of lemon cheese. She was a great wine-maker and the floor of the cupboard which ran underneath the staircase was always well stocked with bottles of mature elderberry, red plum, golden perry, and the light and slightly scented cowslip. Bottles filled with raspberry vinegar stood beside the pots of jam and preserves on the shelves above. As well as these orchard wines, bottles of sloe gin, raisin, wheat and potato wine were made and stored to provide cheer in the years ahead. It was a long and painstaking business, and there were times when it proved to be labour in vain. A bung in a fermenting cask might blow, and a stream of frothy liquid exude from its neck and creep in a sticky stream from under the cupboard door. There would be a loud plop as an insecurely sealed cork left the bottle and hit the ceiling and, occasionally, the staccato crack of a bursting bottle – catastrophes which Aunt dreaded but took in her stride.

Elderberry wine was a cure-all in wintertime and was taken as a medication in hot water with a sprinkling of nutmeg, for chest colds etc. Cowslip wine was for Christmas time and reminded me of our trips into the fields near the river and the hours spent helping Aunt to fill a wicker clothes basket with the fragrant clusters. We then sat down to 'peep' the flowerets from the stalks and drop them into brown pancheons. Raspberry vinegar was heated and poured over plain suet puddings or sipped as a hot cordial at bedtime as a cure for sore throats.

No orchard fruit was allowed to lie on the ground and rot. 'Fallens' were distributed amongst family and friends, made into wine, passed over fences to neighbours or put into old buckets and left outside the gate so that passers-by could help themselves. Gathered fruit from the trees was examined for bruising, wiped clean and stored in wooden trays in the attics. The majority of soft fruits were jammed, bottled or pureed and filled tarts and pies during the dreary winter months.

Summertime brought the 'Sheffielders' with their fishing rods and as one of their favourite stretches of water flowed along on the other side of the bank that abutted the orchard, Aunt often answered the door and found fishermen enquiring about accommodation. Neighbours, too, would bring overflow parties – friends or their own lodgers – knowing there were spare bedrooms at Starling Cottage, and persuaded her to put them up for a night or two. They were friendly, grateful people who laughed when they went upstairs and found they needed long legs to climb up on the down-filled beds, lying like barrage balloons on the ornate brass bedsteads. They fell in love with the shallow wooden staircase which led up to the open attics and were intrigued by the dormer windows and green bottle-glass roofing lights which let the sun's rays stream onto their faces as they lay in bed the next morning.

One or two families returned year after year and I became firm friends with the children of one of them. We played in the sandy hollows along the top of the river bank while their father fished, or scrambled down its other side to the field where the cowslips grew, to play our ball games. On one of these occasions, 'Aunt-next-door' lent us a tennis racquet belonging to my cousin. He was a very good tennis player who went off to matches with several racquets tucked under his arm. We were not to know that the one she passed over the wall was one of his rejects because of a twist in its frame. To us it was a beauty, and I felt a twinge of fear at her trust in us. Nevertheless, we ran off to the fields and spent a glorious afternoon using it in turn, and lobbing balls as hard as we could into the long grasses. We sweated and ran about until we were exhausted and presented ourselves to Aunt around tea-time, thoroughly 'whacked'. She put a bowl of water and towels on a table in the outhouse and tossed a duster to us to wipe the pollen and sand off our shoes before we entered her kitchen. I propped the lovely racquet against the wall of the outhouse in the sun, and we went indoors to have our tea, before returning it to 'Aunt-next-door'.

Uncle Dick left the table first and discovered the catastrophe that had taken place while our backs were turned. We heard his "strewth" and guffaws of laughter. He came into the kitchen, his gold-rimmed spectacles pushed on to his forehead with tears of laughter in his eyes and the racquet held aloft. We were struck dumb with astonishment and dismay. The heat of the sun had bent the racquet nearly double, so that it was a travesty of the elegant thing we had been playing with. Whatever were we to do? 'Aunt-next-door' was unpredictable at the best of times. One or two of us began to cry. Aunt Harriet did not see the funny side either and her look told Uncle he ought to have more sense. She followed him outside and so did we. We stood around, dejected and tearful while he balanced his feet on the buckled rim and rocked his weight in an effort to straighten it, to no avail. There was no way out except to go to 'Aunt-next-door' and tell her that we couldn't help what had happened. It took all of us to do it and, wonder of wonders, she told us it did not matter at all!

My friends took me back to Sheffield with them one year and I found they lived above their father's grocery shop. It stood in a busy street with gutters full of windblown papers and its pavements thronged with people all day long. There was nowhere to play in safety except a small semi-basement area which could only be reached by clambering down a fire escape from the first floor. We played amongst stacks of empty boxes and splintered packing cases, awaiting the dustmen to take them away. I could understand why my friends looked forward to holidays at Starling Cottage and playing with me in the fields.

Chapter 21

A MERRY, MERRY CHRISTMAS

Bonfire night was over and almost forgotten and now we began to think about Christmas plans. All the Wednesday halfpennies and Saturday twopences to come were rashly calculated into a future grand total that never, ever materialised. By the time we sat up in bed together, falling out over the writing of our Christmas present list, we were hard put to make even necessary ends meet, and some friends and relations were doomed to be recipients of our homemade offerings.

Tiny bottles of Californian Poppy and Lily of the Valley perfumes from Piper's Penny Bazaar were to be highlights of Mother's and Aunt Harriet's Christmas morning. Father was easy. He was always astonished to receive a packet of five Woodbines which Mother had been instructed to buy for us and keep well hidden. Uncle Dick, who was an absolute fanatic about washing behind the ears, and who nearly drowned himself in soap and water every time he sluiced himself down at the kitchen sink, was a natural for a pat of Lifebuoy soap.

For weeks past, we had been more easily persuaded to run errands, and the intermittent rewards had been gratefully received, but most of this small fortune had been handed over to Mother, for passing on to the lady who ran the Christmas Chocolate Club. We guarded our green Club cards carefully and the lines of penny and twopenny contributions were spattered with our pencil dots, for we checked and re-checked the grand total after every entry. If we missed the odd week, there was no telltale gap on the card, thanks to Mother, and by the time the chocolate lady brought the wonderful, coloured chocolate book for us to choose from, we were home and dry and dying to select.

One year my sister splurged the whole of her grand total on a two-pound box of King George V Golden Sovereign, but by the time she had worked down to the bottom layer – and been generous handing them round – she was literally sick of King George and his chocolates.

Pre-Christmas shopping with Mother was lovely. Everybody gave her something. The deaf old grocer in the town centre would write down her order and when it came we would find a packet of chocolate biscuits, or a pretty tin full of tea, all for nothing. The butcher was just as kind. He sent our meat and wrapped up beside it was a pound of his fat sausages and a tinselled calendar to hang on the wall. Everyone who served Mother throughout the year produced a little gift. We were often lucky too. A packet of star-shaped biscuits would come our way, and the lady at the sweet shop would find a chocolate cigar or a sugar pig for us to hang on our Christmas tree. It was a time of goodwill which was received by us with surprise and real gratitude.

We looked at the Christmas cards but we did not buy them. They were for those who had more money to spend, but we cherished the ones we received from Granny and the Manchester uncles and aunts from one Christmas to the next. They were carefully slotted into Mother's postcard album and kept us entertained by many a winter's fireside.

Santa's list was no trouble to us as we never thought about making one. Mother listened to our chatter and watched our faces when we went with her to the shops and drew her own conclusions. A skipping rope never went amiss, a whip and top or a hoop and stick were all a joy, and an uncle in Manchester who worked in a rubber factory could usually be relied on to instruct Santa Claus to pop a painted ball into his sack. A *Chatterbox* annual occasionally lay on the counterpane in the half-light of Christmas Day dawn and kept us happy for the year ahead. Once there was a gorgeous cardboard workbox with a pink tulip on its lid and rows of tiny cotton reels and a pair of scissors. Dutch dolls with painted black hair on their wooden heads and bright red circles of paint on their cheeks came to us dressed in minute hand-knitted frocks. There were tubular pencil cases with screw tops, filled with pencils and a dip pen. Such anticipated delights kept us awake long after lights-out on Christmas Eve, and made poor Father in his guise as Santa trot upstairs and down in the vain hope that we had nodded off – at last! We spent Christmas morning by the fire in the front parlour with Father and the little Christmas tree. Nobody minded picking their steps through the 'kelter' on the floor, and as long as we kept ourselves from under Mother's feet, we could do as we liked. She was busy in the other room, cooking the Christmas chicken that Aunt Harriet had given us. We remembered it strutting around in the hen pen, snowy-white and full of itself, and we couldn't help feeling a bit sorry for it now, lying on the dish, trussed up and full of stuffing. Christmas dinner was nearly as exciting as Santa Claus for we never ate chicken during the rest of the year, and although we didn't like Christmas pudding very much, we were willing to swallow a mouthful or two in the hope of finding the silver threepenny piece which we knew was hiding somewhere inside it.

On Boxing Day, as soon as dinner was over, we made ourselves ready for the long walk across town to spend the afternoon and evening with Aunt and Uncle at Starling Cottage. Gaitered and muffled in long scarves tied over our coats and anchored behind our backs with a large safety pin, we set off with our presents for them and with something to play with while we were there. They had no children of their own and we knew that when the tea-time treat was over and the crackers pulled, we should have to behave ourselves with our own toys. The grown-ups settled down to the business of whist or dominoes in the best room which overlooked the orchard, but our mecca was the kitchen with its cheery fire behind the guard and the big snip rug that Aunt had pegged.

We played together and helped ourselves from the apple dish and the sweet tin on the table. The clockwork gramophone with its tin horn and pile of ancient records was to hand and ours to wind and grind to our heart's content. We were at one end of the house and the grown-ups at the other, so nobody got peevish about the din we made. All the same, Uncle's temper was unpredictable and there were times when he forgot it was the season of mirth and merriment.

Games were all very nice if he won, but dominoes that persisted in turning up with the wrong set of spots on them, or cards which wouldn't win tricks more than once in a while, were no joke. He could only stand so much, and if somebody round the table went so far as to sympathise, with tongue in cheek, or were bold enough to laugh outright, away would go the dominoes to all corners of the room and the offending hand of cards were flung on the fire. Aunt would tut and remonstrate and Mother and Father sat tight until the air cooled, then somebody would take the coward's way out and call us in to join the party and break the tension. Sooner or later the two men would vanish up the road for half an hour at The Barge Inn near the sluice gates, while we joined Mother and Aunt with our glasses of diluted cowslip wine, and feasted ourselves on mince pies and tarts. It was cosy sitting in the glow from two rose-coloured glass lamps on the sideboard, and the fire and wine lulled us to a happy drowsiness. It was shattered by the return of the two wanderers. Uncle's puckish face was even redder than usual, and his eyes which he said were 'swimmy' with the light, surveyed us all behind his gold-rimmed spectacles. The plaguey dominoes and obstinate trump cards were all forgotten.

We went out the back with Aunt to spend a penny and then upstairs to bring down our hats and coats, ready to face the long trek home. It was often a bitterly cold journey, icy underfoot, and dark except for a ring of insipid light from a lonely gas lamp or lighted window. The wind that coursed along the river cut into us like a knife as we hurried over the sluice bridge. We often met drunken revellers of both sexes, reeling and singing, oblivious to the weather. We passed some who found that hands and knees were the only mode left to get them home. Mother would snort in disgust and inform the company at large what kind of reception would meet the crawler if he or she belonged to her.

One year, when we were on this homeward agony, we had just crossed the bridge when we met my best friend, Lottie with her mother, father and big sister, Doris. It was nearly eleven o'clock and pouring with rain, and they were on their way to the railway station to catch a late train. They had spent their last Christmas in England with relatives, for they were emigrating to Canada and were due to sail in a few days. Lottie's father and mine had spent many peaceful hours together with rod and line on the banks of the Drains, and our mothers had shared many a worry over the garden fence. Now they were leaving us. We all stood together, feeling sad and lost for the right words to say at such a chance meeting, but at last mothers and fathers shook hands and began to separate. I wanted Lottie to know that I loved her and I wanted her to remember me. I had taken a tin of Huntley & Palmers biscuits, which Santa had left me the night before, to show them to Aunt. Lottie could have it for a keepsake. I ran back to her and pressed it into her hands then came back to Mother and cried for my friend all the way home.

Chapter 22

A LANCASHIRE LASS

Granny Hall lived in Manchester with my father's unmarried brothers and sisters. There was also Rip, the Airedale and Joey the parrot. We sometimes went to see them all when there was a cheap Sunday trip, but this time it wasn't a Sunday and only Father and I climbed onto the train, after kissing my mother and sister 'goodbye'. I had no idea what the Depression was, but I knew Father had not been to work for a long time. Now he had found work to do in Manchester and I was going to keep him company. Mother and my sister had to stay behind "to mind the house". I was nearly seven – a big girl – but I could not help weeping as the train pulled away from the platform and even Father blew his nose very hard once or twice.

It was dark and pouring with rain when we walked from Manchester Central station and boarded a tram in Piccadilly to take us to Granny's house. She didn't know I was coming. Father put me behind him when he rang the doorbell, so that I could jump out and surprise her when she answered it, but Uncle John opened the door. He swept me up in his arms and marched back into the house with me to astonish a ring of faces in the living room.

It was still raining when I opened my eyes the next morning and looked round the strange attic bedroom, from my single bed near the window. Whoever had slept in the double bed on the far side of the room, and I hoped it was Father, had already dressed and gone downstairs. I pulled aside the lace curtain and looked a long way down into two identical rows of paved yards. They were enclosed by high brick walls, with doors which faced each other, all along an equally dreary paved entry. A wet old man and his wet old donkey and cart were coming slowly along from the far end, and it was he who had wakened me with his raucous chant "Raaag-bone, Raaag-bone, Blu'-stone, Brown-stone, Mon-key Brand". His coloured "stones" were chalky substances used to brighten the sills round bay windows and the stone steps leading up to front doors. Monkey Brand was a hard slab of mottled, household soap.

Aunt Una shared my bedroom. She came in, kissed me, and made our beds while I dressed myself. There was only Granny, Joey and Rip in the living room when we went downstairs. Everyone else had already gone to work, including Father. Rip lay full stretch on the hearth rug, warming his belly before the fire. He lifted his head and looked at me as I came through the door and I knew, as if he had said it aloud, that he was my enemy. He got up and walked round me on stiff legs. I sensed jealousy in his eyes and a threat in the ridge of brindled fur along his back. From that first day he knew that he terrified me. He dared me to move past him if he lay on the rug. He sat like a statue in front of my chair, and I sat on my legs until they were numb, but I dare not let them dangle. The only time I felt safe was on Father's knee.

The family loved him but they were worried and he was banished to his kennel unless they were around to keep an eye on me.

The climax came one tea-time when I ran across the room to welcome Father in from work. Rip sprang with a snarl from under the table and sank his teeth into my shoulder as he knocked me down. It was only a flesh wound, but it sealed his fate. Uncle John manhandled him out of the room and the following day Rip went away, but he left me with a life-long fear of dogs.

My days passed slowly in the big, strange house which was three storeys high and had two large cellars. Granny and Aunt Una had plenty to do as there were eight of us to cook for. They were very kind to the quiet little girl who wandered in and out of rooms and along the landings seeking them, but the clock was their master. Joey was the only one with time to waste and he became my confidant and friend. He was very old and rather tatty but his repertoire was as good as ever and included a few expletives learned from Uncle John, whose fingers he bit. It made the aunts blush when he squawked them out in front of their young men. His bright eyes often saw the tears in mine when I sat by him, thinking of Mother and home and wishing I was there. My loneliness during the day worried Granny. She told Father she thought I would be happier if I went to school and though I begged him not to let me go, he thought the company of other children would stop me moping.

Granny knew a schoolgirl who lived in one of the houses just across the Entry. She promised to call for me and see me home safely until I could find my own way. It was not very far to go, but the maze of streets criss-crossing one another and all looking alike, gave me visions of wandering around in them forever. Just in case my new friend forgot to call or ran home without me, Father drew a diagram of the route and slipped it into my coat pocket.

The 'clack-clack' of clogs in the streets was a novel sound to me and I found they made just as much noise in the classroom when my deskmates kicked their feet on the iron frames as they settled in their seats. It was a mill district and clogs were the accepted footwear in millworkers' families. They were hard-wearing and relatively cheap, and the majority of the bigger boys and a few girls wore them. When we came out of school, I noticed that some of the grannies standing around the gate had clogs on too and wore black shawls round their shoulders. What surprised me most of all were the men's cloth caps on their heads. My friend did not wear clogs as her mother thought they were common, but I wished someone would buy me a pair. They were terrible weapons on the feet of an adversary and many a playground kicking match ended in bloody shins and swollen ankles.

I found that my reading ability was above the average of others in the class. They laughed at my round o's and broad a's and at the expression I had been taught to put into reading aloud. Some of the big boys who squatted behind the dustbins at playtime to play cards or smoke fag ends, could hardly read at all and came sniggering into our classroom for further instruction. They pointed at each word with a nicotined finger and laboured and fidgeted and pronounced adjectives under their breath that would have shocked Joey into a moult and the aunts into a fit.

When someone made a smell in my school, we moved along the seat as far from the culprit as possible, nipped our noses or gave him a look, but we kept quiet. When it happened here the offender was pushed off the end of the seat or kicked on his ankles, and always told what he was. If the teacher remonstrated at the fracas, she was soon informed "Well, Miss, he keeps fartin'".

Weekends were the best times, when Father was free. We explored Belle Vue and stayed until it was dark to watch the fireworks. We went for long rides on the top deck of the trams. We visited the Botanical Gardens or spent sunny hours round the lake in the park, feeding the ducks. Sometimes we just sat on a seat and talked about "going home soon".

Some Saturday afternoons were enlivened for me – and for Granny – by the arrival of two boy-cousins who lived a short tram ride away. The yard gate would crash back against the wall as they galloped through it in a race to be first to reach the kitchen. Granny clicked her tongue or rolled her eyes heavenward and stood well back. In they tumbled, panting and grinning their arrival. As a rule they stayed just long enough to pass on messages from their mother and accept Granny's invitation to stay to tea. Then the hustle was reversed and off they went to spend an hour or two in the large park along the road. Granny's tentative suggestion that I might like to go too was received like a cold shower, until they found I could run as fast as them and could field a ball – but was afraid to bat. We met 'the gang' in the park. The first time, my cousins raced ahead to apologise about me and I met huffy backs and unflattering asides, but in the end, so long as I obeyed orders and did not tell tales, I was tolerated.

Granny was well used to her two ravenous visitors and we invariably returned to eggs and chips, fish cakes or something-on-toast. Hands were washed, Grace was said and then the food was eaten without a lot of chatter. Knives and forks had to be held properly and elbows that stuck out were remarked upon and lowered to our sides. Anyone who forgot himself and shovelled food in on his knife blade was warned to be careful or he would become a patient in the hospital 'pig' ward.

So many weekends came and went that I almost lost hope in "going home soon". When, at last, the longed-for letter came to tell Father there was work near home, I burst into tears of relief. I counted the days and then the hours. Granny washed and ironed our clothes and then packed the case. My cousins came with their mother and she gave me half a crown. Aunt Una bought me a pink dress with a blue satin sash and I went with her to have my photograph taken (see page 59). The other aunts gave me a new *Chatterbox* annual. I could not eat or sleep for excitement. Saturday came and Father and I stood at the end of New Lorne Street, waving goodbye to Granny and all the aunts and uncles crowded around her on the front steps, then we turned the corner and caught a tram to the station.

Dear Mother, dear bossy sister, dear Number 10 – how thankful Father and I were to see them again. What laughing and chattering there was in the little living room and what bliss to snuggle into my own bed and be tucked in by Mother.

Chapter 23

FIVE INTO TWO WON'T GO

Naive, ignorant, innocent – any one or, perhaps, all of these labels fitted us who, at almost twelve years of age, still had open minds about the 'stork', the 'gooseberry bush' and the Doctor's 'black bag'. Nobody told us *anything* so there were never any startling revelations whispered amongst us in the school lavatories; boys were just boys and girls were just girls and the word "sex" meant one or the other. We knew that the boys stood up when they 'paid-a-visit' and that we sat down and thought that was all there was to it. If some of my playmates had already reached puberty, I knew nothing about it and I do not suppose they did until the moment it happened; some of them, no doubt, thought they were going to die! I remember one buxom girl being loaded onto a handcart and pushed home, with monotonous regularity, once a month – but no one amongst my friends knew why and we never thought to ask her. Of course, it was noticeable that some of us were beginning to put a great strain on our liberty bodices and that others amongst us were still as flat as boards; the still-deflated may have secretly wondered what it was that they lacked in their diet but, as a rule, we all accepted the vagaries of nature and rarely questioned her discrepancies.

Country children were, no doubt, more knowledgeable through their close contact with field and farm animals, yet even some of them – like me, when I witnessed the birth of the lambs – may not have considered the functions of animal reproduction in connection with those of human births. Ninety-nine per cent of all mothers who realised they were pregnant did their utmost – and succeeded – to keep the secret safe from the rest of the brood until they could present the baby in all its pink and powdered perfection; and that is just how it was with my sister and I when we ran into the house from school, at tea-time, on the day before her seventh birthday. We found we had a new little sister waiting for us upstairs – and I was as dumbfounded as she was.

She was not at all thrilled with such a pre-birthday present, realising that it would monopolise a lot of Mother's attention for a long time to come, and that she would still be up in the bedroom the next day when, normally, she would have been downstairs, presiding over the birthday tea-table. As it was, Father deputised and the birthday tea was prepared and taken upstairs on trays and eaten by her bedside.

Now there were five of us, something had to be done; the little house was getting too crowded for our comfort. The double bed, the dressing table and the marble-topped washstand, the cane-seated chair near the window and the new baby's cot in the corner filled the small front bedroom so that we had to thread our way to get in and out of it. My sister and I were growing up fast and needed more space too; the double bed we shared took up most of the room and its width even prevented us opening the door to its fullest extent. Father and Mother began to talk about seeking a larger rented house. They were not as difficult to obtain then as they had been when we had come to Pinafore Street seven years before. Then, the peace after the Great War was only a few months old and the homecoming of fathers and the reunion of families everywhere, all eager for any place to call their own, made the meanest hovel hard to find and our capture of Number 10 had been something like a miracle.

Dole queues, Means Tests, slumps, a General Strike – these were the bogies that kept families static later on and Mother and Father did not escape. Rent money was hard to find when the English weather ruled the wage packet, as it did Father's. A wet day often meant no pay if the building firm he worked for had no indoor job for him to do; little wonder he called rain that fell on a Sunday "poor man's rain". A prolonged frost or a heavy fall of snow could put him on the dole for several weeks at a time so, although we badly needed a larger house, its rent was the all-important factor in making a decision to accept the key.

When at last we found one, it was another Number Ten, but coincidence did not end there. It also had a one-hole privy, another outside tap sited twenty yards, or more, from the back door and shared with the next-door neighbour, and another 'tunnel' staircase going up between the inner walls of the two downstairs rooms. Nevertheless, these familiar 'refinements' were more than offset by the third bedroom and by the kitchen and walk-in pantry leading from the living-room. Admittedly, the extra bedroom was tiny and only accessible through one of the others and the downstairs front room floor had dry rot beneath its bay window. Nor was Mother overjoyed with the red-tiled floors in the living-room, kitchen and pantry, which she knew would quickly rot any linoleum that was laid upon them and would, otherwise, need washing over daily to keep their colour. The outside 'appurtenances' in the yard consisted of a shared rainwater cistern, a coal-cum-wash-house and the privy. A communal pathway cut across the end of the yard and separated it from a narrow strip of garden that had a dirt-and-cinder path and two leaning wooden clothes-posts, with green mossy heads. It was the fifth house in a row of ten whose small square bay windows protruded to within three feet of the pavement and were separated from it by iron railings and gates.

"Browns Road", said the nameplate, high up on the side wall of the little general shop on the corner. It was a short road, pierced on either side by alleyways that led to other cul-de-sacs and it terminated in a dead end of high wooden-railed fencing that closed off a grass field beyond. We had a job to find it the first time we went to see the house. We left Pinafore Street and walked beside the Drain as far as the stone bridge, then veered to the right and crossed a busy main road and, again keeping company with the Drain, passed a lovely windmill and a row of picturesque almshous-es, eventually turning sharply right near an iron-railed foot-bridge into Hospital Lane. It was a long narrow lane, bear-ing its burden of villas, cottages, almshouses, nursery gar-dens, fish shop, general shop, etc., and stretching them before us to a distant bend, there to meet a residential road. "Walk halfway down," said a lady of whom we asked guid-ance, "you will find Burns Road on the left-hand side."

So we moved in and found ourselves tucked away in a dead-end, halfway down a lane that was, itself, a backwater. Mother hated being there and spoke nostalgically of Pinafore Street, that had led us into town one way and down to the Seabank the other and which was open and airy in comparison. It took many months for her to become reconciled to being "buried alive". School was not "just round the corner" either and she did not find it easy to prise us out of bed so much earlier, nor did we relish turning out in all weathers to trudge such a long way backwards and forwards, several times each day.

In the end, though, both she and we found a silver lining: she, in what proved to be a lifelong friendship with a neighbouring family, and we, when we got to know the eight children who lived in the house next door and the dozens more – some of whom we found we knew already – who emerged every morning from the network of alleyways and joined us in the long trek to school.

HAPPY DAYS AND HEARTBREAK DAYS

A farmer's son relives his 1920s childhood
VICTOR WILLIAM DILWORTH

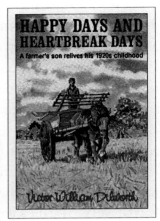

AFTER Victor Dilworth drove by chance through the village where he was born in the 1920s, he started to recall his earliest memories of life on the family farm, Hinstock Grange. In his retirement, as he concentrated on these recollections, they became so real that it felt as though he had been reborn into those times and was actually reliving his experiences. Describing long-gone sights, sounds, smells and emotions, he employs a turn of phrase so evocative and exact that reading this book is like watching a vivid video being played in the mind, 'filmed' through the eyes of a toddler and small boy. The scenes are set in his native Shropshire and also in Cheshire, where he visits the farm and watermill where his father was brought up.

The youngest of the family ('the scratching of the pot'), Victor finds that his hard-working parents have little time for him until he can do some useful work. Affection comes from his big sister, his grandfather and his beloved dog, Rover. Always anxious to learn, he watches the family milking cows, making prize-winning cheese and tending the many animals. He sees lambs being born and under threat of a whack from the cow strap he refrains from touching the baby chicks as they emerge from their shells in the incubator. He helps the farm waggoner to oil the horse-drawn mowing machine and accompanies his father to feed the sheep, on a float pulled by Dolly the pony. He learns about the cycle of life and death on the farm and comes to realise "that all creatures on earth are dependent on each other, just like the strands of a spider's web suspended on a hedgerow in the autumn."

He sets off to school just before his fourth birthday, full of trepidation about the unknown outside world...

ISBN 1 901253 34 1   108pp, A5, colour and b&w photos   **Price £6.99**

Léonie Press, 13 Vale Road, Hartford, Northwich, Cheshire CW8 1PL; tel 01606 75660; fax 01606 77609, e-mail anne@leoniepress.com website: www.leoniepress.com

Elizabeth Anne Galton (1808-1906)

A Well-connected Gentlewoman

Edited by ANDREW MOILLIET

ELIZABETH Anne Galton's mind was as sharp and enquiring in her nineties, when Edward VII was King, as it had been in her youth during the Regency period. Her long life fitted almost exactly into the 19th century and, in the fascinating reminiscences from which this book is taken, she chronicled its changes with an observant eye. She was a devout philanthropic woman, but her strong principles were leavened with a great sense of fun.

A list of her friends, relations and acquaintances reads like a scientific, financial and commercial 'Who's Who'. She was the daughter of an influential Birmingham banker who managed the city's affairs as High Bailiff – today's equivalent of Mayor. Through him she was related to many Quaker families of importance including the Barclays, Frys, Gurneys and Lloyds, in addition to those like the Wedgwoods whose forebears had helped to make the Industrial Revolution.

Elizabeth Anne's brother, Sir Francis Galton FRS, is regarded as the founder of the science of eugenics. Among his other accomplishments he pioneered the use of finger-prints as a method of identification. She and the great Charles Darwin shared a common grandfather, Erasmus Darwin FRS, who was the moving spirit in the famous group of scientists, the Lunar Society of Birmingham – nicknamed the "Lunaticks". These illustrious men and their friends appear in her memoirs in a very human light.

In 1838, Elizabeth Anne attended Queen Victoria's Coronation at Westminster Abbey, which she described at the time as the happiest day of her life. In 1897, as a spritely 89-year-old, she watched Victoria's ("very long") Diamond Jubilee celebration procession as it passed through London.

Her memoirs have been edited by Andrew Moilliet, a descendant of her sister Lucy. There are gems of all kinds on every page, including the defeat of Bonaparte, dancing bears, highwaymen, the first trains, the Great Exhibition of 1851, the 'science' of phrenology, life at a Regency spa, her 'season' as a debutante, the death of George III, a lavish dinner for the Duke of Wellington, his grand public funeral – and the blissful arrival of elastic shoulder-straps for stiffly-corseted women.

ISBN 1 901253 36 8   256pp, A5, 33 b+w illustrations   **Price £10.99**

Léonie Press, 13 Vale Road, Hartford, Northwich, Cheshire CW8 1PL;
tel 01606 75660; fax 01606 77609, e-mail anne@leoniepress.com
website: www.leoniepress.com

127

TALES FROM A SPORTING LIFE

Memories of a Mersey man who made his mark
PERCY YOUD (1879-1963)

TALES FROM A SPORTING LIFE

Percy Youd (1879-1963)
Memories of a Mersey man who made his mark

WHEN Percy Youd was born in Frodsham in 1879, the Manchester Ship Canal was soon to be constructed nearby. He grew up to be a naughty boy who 'wagged off' school, played practical jokes and was banned from his corrugated iron church for ringing its bell with stones shot from his catapult. From an early age, natural ability and a marksman's eye singled him out as an outstanding shot with anything from a muzzle-loader to a 12-bore shotgun. His quarry included game in the Cheshire hills and wildfowl on the Mersey estuary. He was a fearless fist-fighter and an excellent athlete.

Percy worked in the cable factories at Helsby and Prescot. After a few years his bosses asked him to take on a Hotel on the edge of the 'Wire Works' complex and he turned it into a popular and well-known sporting venue.

He later moved to Birkenhead. He was a keen member of the Conservative Club in Ellesmere Port and set up in business in the town as an auctioneer. He led many shooting parties and his marksmanship was the subject of betting.

He organised a 100,000-name petition to try to save his Chinese friend, convicted murderer Lock Ah Tam, from the gallows and claimed friendship with Tory senior politician Selwyn Lloyd.

In old age Percy wrote some of his memories down in a 22,000-word unpunctuated "lump" of vividly descriptive prose which was discovered after his death – including the script of the Frodsham 'soul-caking' play. This book contains the gently edited text, together with family portraits, old photographs and postcards, press cuttings and background information. There is also an account by his daughter of her childhood with him in the 1920s after he abducted her from his estranged wife. Their landlady had a crystal ball and never gave the girl a proper meal.

ISBN 1 901253 30 9   188pp, A5 format, 94 illustrations   **Price: £8.99**

Léonie Press, 13 Vale Road, Hartford, Northwich, Cheshire CW8 1PL;
tel 01606 75660; fax 01606 77609, e-mail anne@leoniepress.com
website: www.leoniepress.com